Cities for a small planet

Copyright © 1997 by Richard Rogers

This edition published in 1998 in the United States of America by Westview Press, 5500 Central Avenue, Boulder, Colorado 80301-2877

First published in 1997 in Great Britain by Faber and Faber Limited, 3 Queen Square, London WC1N 3AU

A CIP record for this book is available from the Library of Congress.
ISBN 0-8133-3553-1

The paper used in this publication meets the requirements of the American National Standard for Permanence of Paper for Printed Library Materials Z39.48-1984.

10   9   8   7   6   5   4   3   2   1

Cities for a small planet
Richard Rogers

edited by Philip Gumuchdjian

Westview Press
A Member of Perseus Books, L.L.C.

Acknowledgements

The beauty of practising architecture is that it is an inclusive experience, an adventure enjoyed with others. I am in debt to many, of whom I can mention only a few here:

To my friend and co-writer Philip Gumuchdjian, who worked with me through the lectures and this book line by line; to Ben Rogers, who made me think and write more clearly; and to Ricky Burdett, who helped define the overall strategy.

To Professors Peter Hall and Edward Pearce; to Herbert Girardet, Roy Porter, Ian Ritchie, Sir Crispin Tickell, Alan Yentob and Ruth Rogers; and to Brian Anson and Dr Anne Power, whose understanding of the problems of the poor has constantly inspired me.

To Pippo Lionni and Bruno Charpentier of L design, who designed the book; to Magnum Photos and Greenpeace, who assisted us in our picture research; and to Anthony Denselow, BBC producer of the Reith Lectures, and Steve Cox. Also to Andrew Wright, Robert Webb, Jo Murtagh, Fiona Charlesworth, Emma England, Martha Fay and all those whose contributions made this book.

Above all to my partners John Young, Marco Goldschmied, Mike Davies, Laurie Abbott and Graham Stirk, whose ideas are freely used in the book and who generously sponsored the work.

Contents

Introduction
by Sir Crispin Tickell

For many people, Richard Rogers's 1995 Reith Lectures came as something of a shock. He made them see cities – their past, their present and their future – in a new light. Thus the familiar became the exotic. Under his tutelage the daily experience of urban living, or the movement in and out of cities with the morning and evening human tides, seemed almost hazardous. At the same time he opened up prospects of choice for the future, and thereby created a marvellous sense of liberation.

The first and most obvious thing about cities is that they are like organisms, sucking in resources and emitting wastes. The larger and more complex they become, the greater their dependence on surrounding areas, and the greater their vulnerability to change around them. They are both our glory and our bane. We are not alone in the natural world in making them. As Lewis Thomas once wrote of ants, 'They are so much like human beings as to be an embarrassment. They farm fungi, raise aphids as livestock, launch armies for wars, use chemical sprays to alarm and confuse their enemies, capture slaves . . . They exchange information ceaselessly. They do everything but watch television.'

Like other successful animals, the human species has learned to adapt to new environments.

But unlike others, humans made a jump from being successful to being a runaway success. They have made this jump because of their ability to adapt environments for their own use in ways that no other animal can match.

It is an ingrained belief that human progress has been, with just one or two blips, upwards and onwards. In fact few trends go in this fashion. All previous urban societies have collapsed. Perhaps the earliest was that of the Harappa culture in the Indus valley some 3500 to 4500 years ago. The destruction of forest cover and removal of topsoil prevented the rise of moisture, even in summer. With sharply diminishing rainfall, declining fertility of soil and rising population, Harappa society lost its natural resource base, and simply collapsed. The same could well have happened in the valleys of the Tigris and Euphrates and in pre-Columbian Mexico, as it is happening in parts of the Sahel belt across Africa today.

The proximate reasons for these collapses are various. But all are subject to three variables: population, environment and resources.

There were perhaps around 10 million humans at the end of the ice age some 12,000 years ago. The introduction of agriculture, the specialisation of human function and the growth of cities caused rapid proliferation. By the time of Thomas Malthus, when the Industrial Revolution had barely started, our numbers stood at around 1 billion.

By 1930 they had risen to 2 billion. They are now around 5.8 billion, and by 2025, short of some catastrophe, they will be 8.5 billion. At present there are more than 90 million new human beings every year, or the equivalent of a new China (at present 1.2 billion) every twelve years.

The steepest growth rate has been in cities. In 1950 29 per cent of the world's population was urban. In 1965 it was 36 per cent, in 1990 50 per cent, and by 2025 it could be at least 60 per cent. The world annual growth rate of urban population between 1965 and 1980 was 2.6 per cent; but between 1980 and 1990 it was 4.5 per cent. Nearly all the current increase is in poor countries, by definition those with the least resources and the lowest capacity to dispose of waste.

It should go without saying that the more people there are, the worse these problems will become. Most resources are renewable, and even those that are non-renewable – for example, fossil fuels – can usually be replaced. A prime problem today is that pressure of consumption can render renewable resources unrenewable, or renewable only after long stretches of time.

Environmental degradation has anyway accelerated. The most conspicuous aspect is land use. According to the United Nations environmental data report of 1993/94, 17 per cent of soils world-wide have been damaged to a greater or lesser extent since 1945.

The quality of the air above has also deteriorated. Air pollution has already reduced US crop production by 5 to 10 per cent, according to US government estimates. It is probably having a still worse effect in Eastern Europe and in China.

By the middle of the next century pressure on food supplies will come from many quarters: so far we have been saved by the green revolution, but the prospects for another are dim. Until recently the main food problem was distribution. That is no longer so. With recent perturbations of the weather as well as constantly increasing demand, the world may be entering a period of scarcity.

World demand for fresh water is at present doubling every twenty years. Yet even if we can husband and make better use of water resources, the available supply has remained broadly the same since the ice age. Cities have to reach further and further for their water sources. It is no wonder that conflict over them is one of the oldest in human history and could be increasingly dangerous in the future.

Evidence of the limits to sinks for our pollutants is all around us. Waste disposal may soon become as big a problem as consumption of resources. Bursting landfill sites across the industrial world, transboundary shipment of hazardous wastes, and the increasing prevalence of contamination of the groundwater we depend upon, are all reminders that the capacity of the land to absorb waste products is not unlimited.

In the atmosphere acid precipitation is a problem for those down-wind of industry; but it is essentially local in character and can be solved if there is political will to solve it. Depletion of the ozone layer is more serious. Damage to the human metabolism may seem alarming to us, but the more fundamental problem could be the effects on other organisms, not least phytoplankton in the oceans.

Then there are the prospects of human-induced climate change. Usually change takes place so slowly that we do not notice it. Animals, plants and other forms of life have time to adapt or migrate. The Thames valley is an example. 130,000 years ago it was the habitat of swamp-loving hippos; 18,000 years ago reindeer and mammoth roamed the tundra not far from the ice sheet which weighed on the land to the north; and only 900 years ago the French were trying to close down vineyards in southern England which were too competitive.

The last 12,000 years have been a period of relatively stable climate. Even before the Industrial Revolution, and as far back as the Bronze Age, there were variations in local climates due to changes in land use, in particular deforestation. But since the Industrial Revolution began around 250 years ago, we have through our activities brought about the prospect of global changes, or alterations in whole weather systems. Everything is speeding up. Apart from what we have done to the land (in Britain stone, brick and tarmac cover around 10 per cent of the total), humans have been changing the chemistry of the atmosphere through combustion of fossil fuels and living matter, in particular forest burning.

Although some scientific uncertainties remain, we now seem set on a course of global climate change which will have two major effects. First are changes which could cause rain to fall where it rarely fell before, or rain not to fall where it had previously been abundant. It may be warmer or it may be cooler, although the world as a whole seems set for a rise in average temperatures. Such changes have often happened in the past. The second effect is on sea levels. At present sea levels are rising by between 1.5 and 2 millimetres a year. But if current melting of land ice were to accelerate, the rise in sea levels could accelerate with an overall rise of half a metre before the end of the next century.

Last there are the issues arising from the destruction of other forms of life. Such destruction is of an order of magnitude comparable to that brought about by the impacts of objects from outer space. The last major one ended the dominance of the dinosaur family 65 million years ago. When the archaeologists of the future look at the deposits of the last quarter millennium, they will find a biological discontinuity as big as any in the past. They will expose a richness not of fossils but of plastic bags and other human refuse. The effects on the life-support system of the planet cannot yet be measured.

So there is an accumulation and combination of formidable hazards, each driven to a greater or lesser degree by human population increase and urban growth.

In the evolution of human behaviour from hunter-gatherers to farmers and eventually citizens, cities have come to represent a specialisation of human functions. Richard Rogers will show how they represent a value added to human life. Yet cities bring all the hazards together in acute form. Human existence can be at its most degraded in cities and their surrounding shanty towns. Until the last century cities were generally seen as dangerous places. Death rates exceeded birth rates, and cities could maintain themselves only by attracting people from outside. Cities and their support systems create an environment of their own. It is increasingly in peril.

In two of his chapters, Richard Rogers examines the culture of cities and their prospects for sustainability. As collective organisms, they are as vulnerable as any other to change. There are certain obvious pressure points which we could feel very soon, for example supplies of food, water and other physical resources. But lurking behind them are others. Here are one or two examples.

More people, in or out of cities, means more pressure on the environment. It also means more refugees. In 1978 there were fewer than 6 million refugees, on a restricted definition of those fleeing from political, ethnic or religious persecution; by 1995 the figure had risen to over 22 million. These figures do not include environmental refugees, some moving across frontiers, other displaced within them, but depending on their definition the number could be more than another 22 million. Much of the impact of this flow of human beings will be in and around cities.

A rise in sea levels could disrupt the lives of the huge populations living on or near a coastline, or along an estuary. The effect would be compounded by storm surges and the extreme events – storms, droughts, hurricanes and the rest – which we must expect with climate change.

We must also expect changes in patterns of disease. Temperature and moisture greatly affect the life cycles of micro-organisms, from insects through bacteria to viruses. They therefore directly affect human and other animal health. We are already seeing a remarkable return of certain diseases whose agents have become resistant to modern drugs. Populations debilitated for other reasons will be particularly vulnerable. We must also reckon with problems arising from drainage and sewage disposal. Again, the crowded conditions of urban life make cities particularly vulnerable.

A less obvious pressure point is the consequences for cities of the destruction of other forms of life.

Reduction of their diversity affects food supplies (already heavily dependent on a few genetic strains) and medicine (heavily dependent on plant and animal sources). But more important are the ecological benefits: we rely on forests and vegetation to produce soil, to hold it together and to regulate water supplies by preserving catchment basins, recharging groundwater and buffering extreme conditions; we rely on soils to be fertile and to break down pollutants; and we rely on nutrients for recycling and disposal of waste. There is no conceivable substitute for these natural services, and all of them constitute parts of the urban support system. If we tamper with them, the cost could be immeasurable.

Cities also face problems from within themselves. Richard Rogers well brings out the main factors. Nearly all cities were once towns, and nearly all towns were once villages. The bigger communities become, the greater their loss of social coherence. Such cities as London, which is still in many ways a combination of villages with a grand centre, are better to live in than the agglomerations divided by function and lacking human dimension. Los Angeles has been rightly called the Nowhere City. Clusters of huge concrete stalagmites are deeply oppressive to the spirit. Some planners still long to create ghettos in the shape of commercial districts, industrial districts, dormitory districts, shopping districts and the rest without realising the social cost for the individual. I sometimes think that the good mental health of citizens suggests that we should go back to the notion of city walls to preserve the coherence of urban life within and prevent the destruction of it from without. But the gates must always be kept open.

If these factors are not enough, cities are now suffering from the dagger wounds caused by the intrusive, splitting effects of roads to carry everyone's favourite and most convenient toy, the motor car. Richard Rogers examines the necessary balance between public and private transport, the corrosive effects of the priority we have given the car over the last fifty years, and the nature and variety of our dependence on it. Government research has shown that 19 million people a year in Britain are exposed to air pollution levels in excess of international guidelines as a result of the growth in traffic and industry.

This accumulation of issues raises huge problems for governance. We are already undergoing a kind of crisis of authority. Increasingly we have to ask ourselves, can governments cope? Certainly national sovereignty is not what it was. World-wide there is a switch in authority: upwards to international institutions to cope with global problems (even if most remain poorly equipped to do so); downwards to local authorities, local organizations and communities; and sideways to citizens in direct communication with each other through the marvels of information technology anywhere in the world.

Yet we still live in a world in which governments are the critical factor. Public awareness of such issues has greatly increased over the last quarter century, but few people have yet drawn the kind of radical conclusions which are now needed. Most change comes through an accumulation of small steps, followed by an occasional stumbling, then a big step, followed by more small steps. Progress is therefore slow. As Lord Keynes once remarked, it is far easier to take in a new idea than to get rid of an old one. We have a lot of old ones to get rid of.

Certain, mostly economic, principles have become common currency. It is for example agreed at least in theory that the polluter should pay. There is likewise agreement on the precautionary principle, which means that we should not only take care but also not allow uncertainty to obstruct preventive action when it seems necessary. There is also a kind of woolly agreement on a third principle: that environmental considerations should be at the heart of decision-making at whatever level.

Application of these principles should persuade governments to do what makes sense for reasons other than any single factor. Leadership in this respect is essential. But so also is pressure from below from a public educated in the issues and intolerant of shabby compromises.

Sometimes I am asked whether I am an optimist or a pessimist. My reply is that I am an optimist of the intellect because there are ways of managing or at least mitigating the severity of most of the problems that confront us. But I am a pessimist of the will because I doubt whether mere reason is enough. Sometimes we need a jolt, even a catastrophe, to focus our minds and make us readier to accept change. Catastrophe is not the ideal precursor of wise policy making. But without it, it is sometimes hard to see whether we are capable of the changes in fundamental values and aspirations which are indispensable.

Richard Rogers's book is a message of hope. He shows how the equitable – above all, compact – city is pluralist and integrated, diverse and coherent. All of us know that there is something wrong which could become more wrong if we do not look towards a different kind of city in the future. If the ants can work out the right size, character and function for their cities, we should be able to do the same for ours. The result should be, in Richard Rogers's words, a dense and many-centred city, a city of overlapping activity, an ecological city, a city of easy contact, an equitable city, an open city, and not least a beautiful city in which art, architecture and landscape can move and satisfy the human spirit. Richard Rogers shows how it can be done.

1   The culture of cities

To begin our position-fixing aboard our Spaceship Earth we must first acknowledge that the abundance of immediately consumable, obviously desirable or utterly essential resources have been sufficient until now to allow us to carry on despite our ignorance. Being eventually exhaustible and spoilable, they have been adequate only up to this critical moment. This cushion-for-error of humanity's survival and growth up to now was apparently provided just as a bird inside of the egg is provided with liquid nutriment to develop it to a certain point.

Buckminster Fuller,
Operation Manual for Planet Earth

1 In 1957 the first satellite was launched into orbit. It gave us a vantage point from which we could look at ourselves and signalled the beginning of a new global consciousness, a dramatic change in our relationship with the planet. Seen from space, the beauty of the earth's biosphere is striking – but so also is its fragility. The plumes of pollution, the wounds of deforestation, the scars of industrialisation and the sprawl of our cities are all evidence that in our quest for wealth we are systematically plundering every aspect of our life-support system.

The survival of society has always depended on safeguarding the equilibrium between the variables of population, resources and environment. The neglect of this principle had disastrous and fatal consequences for civilisations of the past. We too are subject to the controlling laws of survival, but unlike them we are the first to be a global civilisation and therefore the first to have ever faced a simultaneous and world-wide expansion of population, depletion of natural resources and erosion of the environment.

Above us as I write, 400 or so satellites, equipped with weather instruments, study coastal, ocean and polar processes, constantly beaming back scans of vegetation and atmosphere, plotting the effects of pollution and erosion. Their data plays a crucial role providing insights into changing geological patterns, global warming and the depletion of the ozone layer. They are witnessing the creation of an environmental catastrophe of a magnitude never before faced by humankind. The exact long-term results of current levels of consumption are not yet clear, but given the scientific uncertainty concerning their precise effects my contention is that we must apply the 'precautionary principle' and ensure that action be taken to safeguard the survival of our species on this planet.

It is a shocking revelation, especially to an architect, that it is our cities that are driving this environmental crisis. In 1900 only one-tenth of the world's population lived in cities. Today, for the first time in history, half the population lives in cities and in thirty years' time it may rise to as much as three-quarters. The urban population is increasing at a rate of a quarter of a million people per day – roughly the equivalent of a new London every month. The world-wide growth of urban populations and grossly inefficient patterns of living are accelerating the rate of increase of pollution and erosion.

It is ironic that mankind's habitat – our cities – is the major destroyer of the ecosystem and the greatest threat to humankind's survival on the planet. In the United States, pollution from cities has already reduced crop production by almost 10 per cent. In Japan, waste dumped by Tokyo city amounts to an estimated twenty million tons every year, waste that has already saturated the entire Tokyo bay. Mexico City is literally drinking its two rivers dry, while London's massive traffic congestion causes greater air pollution today than did the burning of coal in the pre-1956 Clean Air Act period. Cities generate the majority of greenhouse gases, and respected establishment figures such as Sir John Houghton, chair of the United Nations advisory panel on Climate Change, now warn of the disastrous likely effects of current levels of greenhouse gas production.

While the need for cities and the inevitability of their continued growth will not diminish, city living *per se* need not lead to civilisation's self-destruction. I passionately believe that the arts of architecture and city planning could be evolved to provide crucial tools for safeguarding our future, creating cities that provide sustainable and civilising environments. This book will attempt to demonstrate that future cities could provide the springboard for restoring humanity's harmony with its environment.

My cause for optimism is derived from three factors: the spread of ecological awareness, of communications technology and of

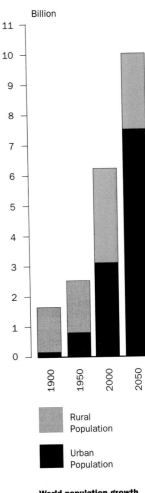

World population growth

automated production. All are contributing conditions for the development of an environmentally aware and socially responsible post-industrial urban culture. Throughout the world, scientists, philosophers, economists, politicians, planners, artists and citizens are increasingly demanding that the global perspective be integrated into strategies for the future. The United Nations report, *Our Common Future*, proposed the concept of 'sustainable development' as the backbone of global economic policy: we should aim to meet our present needs without compromising future generations, and we should actively direct our development in favour of the world's majority – the poor.

The core of this concept of sustainability is the redefining of wealth to include natural capital: clean air, fresh water, an effective ozone layer, a clean sea, fertile land and the abundant diversity of species. The means proposed to ensure the protection of this natural capital are regulations and, most importantly, an appropriate pricing of the market's use of natural capital, an asset that had been previously considered limitless and therefore cost-free. The ultimate aim of sustainable economic development is to leave to future generations a stock of natural capital that equals or ideally exceeds our own inheritance.

Nowhere is the implementation of 'sustainability' more potent and more beneficial than in the city. In fact, the benefits to be derived from this approach are potentially so great that environmental sustainability should become the guiding principle of modern urban design.

If cities are undermining the ecological balance of the planet, it is our patterns of social and economic behaviour that are the root cause of their development in ways that produce environmental imbalance. In both developed and developing worlds the 'carrying' capacity of

cities is being stretched to their limit. Cities are increasing in size and at such a rate that conventional patterns of accommodating urban growth have become obsolete. In the developed world the migration of people and activities from city centres to the dream world of suburbia has led to massive suburban development, wide-spread road-building, increased car use, congestion and pollution – best exemplified in the cities of the Western USA like Phoenix and Las Vegas. Meanwhile, in the fast-growing economies of the developing world, new cities are being built at a phenomenal rate and density with little thought for future environmental or social impact. World-wide, there is a mass migration of the rural poor to these new consumerist cities. Everywhere the situation of the poor is largely overlooked. In the developed world the poor fall out of the consumer society and are abandoned and isolated in the inner-city ghettos, while in the developing cities the poor are relegated to the squalor of the swelling shanty towns. 'Unofficial' or illegal residents regularly outnumber the official ones.

Reckless urban sprawl

◀ Phoenix, Arizona, now occupies a territory as vast as that of sprawling Los Angeles. Its population is just one-third as great.
David Hurn – Magnum

Cities are producing disastrous social instability that is further driving environmental decline. Despite global increases in wealth that far outpace increases in population, the world's poor are growing in number and in poverty. Many of these poor are living in the most squalid environments, exposed to extremes of environmental poverty and perpetuating the cycle of erosion and pollution. Cities are destined to house a larger and larger proportion of the world's poor. It should come as no surprise that societies and cities that lack basic equity suffer intense social deprivation and create greater environmental damage – environmental and social issues are interlocked.

Poverty, unemployment, ill-health, poor education, conflict – in short, social injustice in all its forms – undermine a city's capacity to be environmentally sustainable. Cities that have experienced civil war, such as Beirut; that suffer from severe poverty, such as Bombay; that have alienated large sections of their population from mainstream life, such as Los Angeles; or that pursue profit as their only motive, such as São Paulo, damage the environment to the detriment of all. There can be no urban harmony or real environmental improvements without basic human rights and peace.

Cities throughout the rich, developed world contain communities that are experiencing intense social deprivation, but it is in the rapidly expanding cities of the developing world that the crisis of the poor is expanding all the faster. If unchecked, the ecological and social problems of these cities will soon dominate the human scene. The idea that the rich few can continue to turn their backs on the pollution and poverty of these cities and operate in comfortable isolation from these seats of desolation is short-sighted in the extreme. Lack of basic equity is the constant force undermining attempts to harmonise society and humanise its cities.

Beyond providing opportunities for employment and wealth, cities provide the physical framework for an urban community. In recent decades and throughout the world the public realm of cities, the people's spaces between buildings, has been neglected or eroded. This process has increased the polarisation of society and created further poverty and alienation. New concepts of urban planning that integrate social responsibilities are needed. Cities have grown and changed into such complex and unmanageable structures that it is hard to remember that they exist first and foremost to satisfy the human and social needs of communities. In fact they generally fail to be seen in this way. If you ask people what they think of cities they are more likely to talk about buildings and cars than streets and squares. If you ask them about city life, they are more likely to talk about alienation, isolation, fear of crime or congestion and pollution than about community, participation, animation, beauty or pleasure.

They will probably say that the concepts 'city' and 'quality of life' are incompatible. In the developed world this conflict is driving citizens into the seclusion of private guarded territories, segregating rich from poor and stripping citizenship of its very meaning.

The city has been viewed as an arena for consumerism. Political and commercial expediency has shifted the emphasis of urban development from meeting the broad social needs of the community to meeting the circumscribed needs of individuals. The pursuit of this narrow objective has sapped the city of its vitality. The complexity of 'community' has been untangled and public life has been dissected into individual components. Paradoxically, in this global age of rising democracy, cities are increasingly polarising society into segregated communities.

The result of this trend is the decline of the vitality of our urban spaces. The political theorist Michael Walzer has classified urban space into two distinct groups: 'single-minded' and 'open-minded' spaces. 'Single-minded' describes a concept of urban space that fulfils a single function and is generally the consequence of decisions by old-guard planners or developers. 'Open-minded' is conceived as multifunctional and has evolved or been designed for a variety of uses in which everyone can participate. The residential suburb, the housing estate, the business district, the industrial zone, the car park, underpass, ring-road, shopping mall, even the car itself provide 'single-minded' spaces. But the busy square, the lively street, the market, the park, the pavement café are 'open-minded'. When we are in the first type of spaces we are generally in a hurry, but in the 'open-minded' places we are readier to meet people's gaze and to participate.

Both categories have a role to play in the city. Single-minded spaces cater to our very modern craving for private consumption and autonomy. They are very efficient, in those terms. In contrast, 'open-minded' places give us something in common: they bring diverse sections of society together and breed a sense of tolerance, awareness, identity and mutual respect.

My point, however, is that in the process of designing cities to meet the inexorable patterns of private demand we have seen the former category eclipsing the latter. Open-mindedness has given way to single-mindedness and in its wake we are witnessing the destruction of the very idea of the inclusive city.

The emphasis is now on selfishness and separation rather than contact and community. In the new kinds of urban development, the activities that traditionally overlapped are organised for the purpose of maximising profit for developers or retailers. Businesses are isolated and grouped into business parks; shops are grouped in shopping centres with theatre-set 'streets' built into them; homes are grouped into residential suburbs and housing estates. Inevitably, the streets and squares of this counterfeit public domain lack the diversity, vitality and humanity of everyday city life. Worse still, the existing streets of the city are drained of commercial life and become little more than a no-man's-land for scurrying pedestrians or sealed private cars. People today do value convenience but they also long for genuine public life, and the crowds that pack city centres on weekends testify to this.

The disappearance of 'open-minded' public space is not simply a cause for regret: it can generate dire social consequences launching a spiral of decline. As the vibrancy of public spaces diminishes we lose the habit of participating in street life. The natural policing of streets that comes from the presence of people needs to be replaced by 'security' and the city itself becomes less hospitable and more alienating. Soon our public spaces are perceived as downright dangerous, and fear enters the scene.

In response, activities become ever more territorial. The street market becomes less attractive than the secured shopping mall, the university district becomes the closed campus; and as this process spreads through the city the open-minded public domain retreats. People with wealth bar themselves in or move out of the city. In these closed, privatised spaces, the poor are forbidden to enter, guards stand at the gate. Those without money are equivalent to those without a passport, a class to be banished. Citizenship – the notion of shared responsibility for one's environment – disappears, and city life becomes a two-tier structure, with the rich in protected enclaves and the poor trapped in inner-city ghettos or, as in the developing world, squalid shanty towns. We created cities to celebrate what we have in common. Now they are designed to keep us apart.

The sprawling cities of the USA, with their inner-city ghettos, heavily policed middle-class dormitories, shopping centres and business parks, show this divisive tendency most clearly. The Californian writer Mike Davis describes how Los Angeles, the scene of repeated riots in recent decades, has grown more and more segregated, even militarised.

Starting at the outskirts there is the Toxic Rim, a circle of giant garbage landfill, radioactive waste dumps and polluting industries. Moving inwards you pass so-called gated or privately patrolled residential suburbs and a zone of self-policing lower middle-class homes, until you reach a free-fire downtown area of ghettos and gangs. Here, the Ramparts Division of the Los Angeles police regularly investigate more murders than any other local police department in the country. Finally, beyond this no-go area lies the business district itself. In parts of this area, TV cameras and security devices screen almost every passing pedestrian.

A street for the rich

▲ Security passes gain
access to an air-conditioned
subterranean walkway for
Houston's downtown office
workers and shoppers, leaving
the poor to inhabit the
polluted streets above.
Simon Norfolk,
The Independent

A street for the poor

◄ Fear City, North
Philadelphia 1989, Corner of
Somerset and A streets, one
of the city's major drug-dealing
corners. A gang of children
peddle crack.
Eugene Richards, Magnum

At the touch of a button, access is blocked, bullet-proof screens are activated, bomb-proof shutters roll down. The appearance of the 'wrong sort of person' triggers a quiet panic. Video cameras turn on their mounts. Security guards adjust their belts. A new type of citadel has emerged which relies not only on physical boundaries, high fences, barbed wire and imposing gates but increasingly on invisible electronic hardware.

In LA the car has become the mobile fortress. Tinted windows disguise the identity of passengers, bullet-proof glass protects from armed attack, doors can in an instant be centrally locked from within, creating ever greater alienation of the individual from the city.

The situation in Houston is almost as disturbing. An entire network of underground streets – more than six miles long – has been excavated beneath the city's downtown business district. This glitzy maze, called with unintended irony the 'connection system', is entirely private. You cannot gain admittance to it from the street, but only through the marble lobbies of the banks and oil companies that dominate Houston. The result is the creation of yet another kind of urban ghetto. The car-choked streets are left to the poor and unemployed, while the wealthy workers shop and do business in air-conditioned comfort and security.

Although British or European cities have not yet gone this far, many display similar tendencies writ small. We too have seen a retreat to the suburbs and growing inner-city poverty, an increasing reliance on private security and private transport, the proliferation of single-minded spaces. Any attempt to redress the situation must depend on mobilising the participation of individuals and their sense of belonging to the city. It is the individual's commitment to their city which is so absolutely central to achieving sustainability. Civic beauty is the result of the social and cultural commitment of the communities of an urban society. It is a dynamic force that colours all aspects of city life down to the design of its buildings.

I passionately believe in the importance of citizenship and the liveliness and humanity it stimulates. It manifests itself in planned large-scale civic gestures but also in the small scale and the spontaneous. Together they create the rich diversity of city life. Cities remain the great demographic magnets of our time because they facilitate work and are the seedbeds of our cultural development. Cities are centres of communication, learning and complex commercial enterprises; they house huge concentrations of families; they focus and condense physical, intellectual and creative energy. They are places of hugely diversified activities and functions: exhibitions and demonstrations, bars and cathedrals, shops and opera houses. I love their combination of ages, races, cultures and activities, the mix of community and anonymity, familiarity and surprise, even their sense of dangerous excitement. I enjoy their grand spaces as well as the animation that simple pavement cafés bring to the street, the informal liveliness of the public square, the mixture of workplaces, shops and homes that make living neighbourhoods.

Strolling through Europe's great public spaces – the covered Galleria in Milan, the Ramblas in Barcelona, the parks of London or the everyday public spaces of markets and local neighbourhoods – I feel part of the community of the city. The Italians even have a word which describes the way men, women and children interact with the public space of their city as they stroll on their streets and squares in the evening: they call it *la passeggiata*.

When the Parisian authorities agreed to let us give half the site they had set aside for the Pompidou Centre to a public piazza they were encouraging exactly this type of citizenship. The idea of integrating a bustling public square into the Pompidou Centre project had come from our experience of historic public spaces, such as Jamaa El Afna in Marrakech, Piazza San Marco in Venice and the Campo at the heart of Siena, scene of the Palio horse race. To my great delight the relationship between building and public space, between the Centre and the Place Beaubourg, has created a place teeming with public life and has regenerated the areas around it.

Active citizenship and vibrant urban life are essential components of a good city and of civic identity. To restore these where they are lacking, citizens must be involved in the evolution of their cities. They must feel that public space is in their communal ownership and responsibility. From the modest back street to the grand civic square these spaces belong to the citizen and make up the totality of the public domain, a public institution in its own right which like any other can enhance or frustrate our urban existence. The public domain is the theatre of an urban culture. It is where citizenship is enacted, it is the glue that can bind an urban society.

Cities can only reflect the values, commitment and resolve of the societies which they contain. The success of a city therefore depends on its inhabitants, their government and the priority both give to maintaining a humane urban environment. The Athenians of ancient Greece recognised the importance of their city and the role it played in encouraging the moral and intellectual democracy of their times. The agora, the temples, the stadium, the theatre and the public spaces between them were both the magnificent artistic expression of Hellenic culture and the catalyst for its rich humanist development. The commitment to the interdependence of built form and ideals was captured in the oath pledged by new citizens: 'We will leave this city not less but greater, better and more beautiful than it was left to us.' Quality of urban environment defines quality of life for citizens. The relation between city and civic harmony is well established.

Vitruvius, Leonardo da Vinci, Thomas Jefferson, Ebenezer Howard, Le Corbusier, Frank Lloyd Wright, Buckminster Fuller and others proposed ideal cities that they imagined would create ideal societies – cities that would encourage better citizenship and would enable society to overcome its traumas. While such single-minded visions of cities are no longer relevant to the diversity and complexity of modern society, these architectural attempts at Utopia should remind us that, in a democratic age, contemporary architecture and planning might be expected to express our common philosophical and social values. But in fact, most recent transformations of cities reflect society's commitment to the pursuit of personal wealth. Wealth has become an end in itself rather than a means of achieving broader social goals.

The construction of our habitat continues to be dominated by market forces and short-term financial imperatives. Not surprisingly, this has produced spectacularly chaotic results. It astounds me that the built environment in so many places remains an incidental political issue. Cities are the cradle of civilisation, the condensers and engines of our cultural development. Putting the culture of cities back on the political agenda is critical, for while they might be places where life is at its most precarious, cities can also fundamentally inspire. This is the dichotomy of the city: its potential to brutalise and its potential to civilise.

A new form of citizenship must be evolved that responds to the needs of a modern city. Greater emphasis on citizen participation and better leadership are vital. Involving communities in decision-making requires that the built environment become a standard part of education, and a major component of our National Curriculum. Teaching children about their everyday urban environment equips them to participate in the process of respecting and improving the city. Cities themselves can be a great tool, a live laboratory for education. Environmental sustainability should be at the core of subjects taught – a theme linking physics, biology, art and history. We must make funds available to interest and inform the public. We must teach good citizenship to young and old, and listen to citizens. Much of our future 'quality of life' depends on getting this right.

Should people be demoralised by the apparently insurmountable task of gaining democratic control of their cities, there are encouraging examples from around the world. In many places, the city, in its many aspects from ecology to architecture, is an established issue of public debate and electioneering, a sharp contrast to its neglect in Britain.

President François Mitterrand stated that 'culture', and in particular architecture, was the fourth most important voting issue in France (I dread to think how high British politicians would rank culture). In Britain we are perhaps aware only of major initiatives such as the Grand Projects of Paris, but these are just the tip of the iceberg. In France there is a competition for each and every government building, be it a public housing project, a school, a post office, a local square, a park or an entire new town. All local competitions of any significance are decided by a jury comprised of the mayor, a representative of the users, members of the local community, technical experts and architects. There are small competitions designed to encourage young talent as well as major international competitions (often involving the President himself) designed to ensure that France is home to the best of international architecture.

Contrast this with the situation in Britain, where taxpayers spend £4 billion annually on their public buildings and yet central government has had no architectural policy. In 1992 we held ten public design competitions to France's 2,000. Britons complain about their architecture, yet they have a generation of talented young architects who almost without exception have received no public commissions in this country. It is maddening to watch real talent being squandered today and a mediocre architectural heritage left for tomorrow.

Curitiba, a rapidly expanding city in Brazil, succeeded, thanks to far-sighted leadership and public participation, in tackling its problems of growth and consolidation. As I will describe later, they have pursued myriad policies aimed at increasing environmental and social awareness, covering everything from education to commerce, transport to planning. As a result, citizens feel that they own their city and are responsible for its future.

Rotterdam provides an example of concerted government-sponsored but community-oriented development. A strategic plan for the entire city defines the principle directions in which the community wish to see their city grow. The conversion of their docklands is the subject of continuous study, debate and collaboration. The majority of land in and around the city is publicly owned and can be given to the community when and where the need arises rather than when someone can afford to buy a site. The city aims to grow like a cell structure, splitting and replicating into mixed neighbourhoods of three to five thousand people with workplaces, schools, shops and housing. At least a third of each new community consists of overflow from neighbouring communities, which ensures the social coherence of the whole. In this way, Rotterdam avoids dividing itself into segregated zones and isolated communities.

In Spain, the end of Franco's rule was followed by the election of city mayors, and in Barcelona strong mayoral leadership backed by popular support totally transformed the city. The Mayor, Pascal Maragal, and his Minister of Culture, the architect Oriel Bohigas, used the hosting of the 1992 Olympics as a catalyst for visionary reform that went much further than the provision of Olympic facilities. It included the establishment of a strategic masterplan for the entire city, the refurbishment of streets and, significantly, the creation of 150 new public squares. They called upon some of the world's leading architects to implement the most ambitious of all the city's redevelopment plans: the conversion of its defunct industrial dock area that had separated the city from the sea, a waterside area typical of coastal industrial cities throughout the world. The result is that the city has been reconnected to the sea along a huge stretch of coast. Beyond specific projects, Maragal has created an atmosphere in which the private sector is willing to conform to popular public leadership, because developers can both see the overall benefit of the long-term improvement of the city and recognise the importance of public interest. By these democratic processes Barcelona has been transformed into a world-class city, a place where people long to visit, work and live.

The cities of San Francisco, Seattle and Portland have integrated public participation in urban planning into their electoral system. In local elections, you don't just choose a candidate, you have the opportunity to make decisions about your own surroundings: How much office space should be allowed? Which regeneration plan is best? What transportation strategy to adopt? The inhabitants of these cities therefore feel they have involvement and control over their city's destiny.

The above approaches illustrate how urban societies are evolving strategies tailored to their specific culture and needs. In each of these cities there is a fundamental assumption that citizens have a say in the shaping of their cities. They emphatically prove that public participation and genuine government commitment can transform the physical and social fabric of our cities.

I have touched upon some of the problems facing contemporary cities and have illustrated how citizens' commitment can contribute to improving the situation. In parallel we must pursue ever more decisively the development of technologies and innovations that protect our ecology and humanise our cities.

Humankind's capacity to transmit accumulated knowledge from generation to generation, to anticipate and to solve problems, has been its greatest asset. I find it amazing and tremendously inspiring that only a hundred typical lifespans separate our present age, which can build a city in space, from the age which saw the first cities built along the Euphrates and the Tigris.

Technology and our ability to predict have transformed our world, and often in the face of appalling odds. In 1798 the economist Malthus warned that, according to his calculations, the rate of increase in the world population was exceeding the capacity of the earth to feed future generations. He was proved wrong because he had reckoned without the remarkable potential of technology. In the hundred years following his ominous prediction, the population of Britain quadrupled, but technological advances brought a fourteen-fold increase in agricultural production. Nowadays technology develops ever faster and offers even greater opportunities. There were only two lifespans between the invention of the bicycle and that of space travel; and less than half a lifespan between the invention of the first electronic computer and the development of the information superhighway.

In his compelling analysis of modernity in the nineteenth and twentieth centuries, Marshall Berman reminds us of the challenge to traditional social, economic and religious values that accompanies this technological evolution. He quotes from Marx's vivid description of the modern condition:

All fixed, fast-frozen relations, with their train of ancient and venerable prejudices and opinions, are swept away, all new-formed ones become antiquated before they can ossify. All that is solid melts into air, all that is holy is profaned, and men at last are forced to face the real conditions of their lives and their relations with their fellow men.

Embracing change carries uncertainty and risk. The power to transform and change both ourselves and the the world defines our modern condition. The thirst for what we can achieve is balanced by the awareness of our ability to destroy. To be modern, therefore, is to live this life of paradox – this is the Faustian bargain that Berman so brilliantly exposes.

In this maelstrom, the laws of the market have taken hold. But the 'invisible hand' of the market is a force of neither nature nor man. Society, in the form of its governments and other institutions, has the responsibility to focus the dynamic of modern life, to direct the application of new technology, to confront old values with new. The city is the embodiment of society; its form must be continuously viewed against our social objectives. The problems of today's cities are not the result of rampant technological development, but of its rampant misapplication.

The speed of technological change and above all the speed and breadth of its dissemination provides modern society with its greatest potential power. The United Nations Development Agency estimates that in the next thirty years as many people will be seeking a formal education qualification as have done so since the beginning of civilisation. Robotics place our generation in a position to reap the benefit of more wealth per capita with less labour. For the first time since the industrial revolution, work is taking up less of our lives. Robotics, education, medicine, global communications – all manifestations of our technological development – provide the conditions for the development of a new form of creative citizenship that generates wealth for society without breaching the limits of our environment's sustainability.

The challenge we face is to move from a system that exploits technological development for pure profit to one that has sustainable objectives. Making cities sustainable demands fundamental changes in human behaviour, in the practice of government, commerce, architecture and city planning. The developer who builds for purely commercial returns, with no commitment to the city's environment nor to the quality of life of its citizens, is misusing technology. So too is the planner who drives a motorway through the middle of a city without regard for the broader environmental or social issues.

I am wild about technology but not about technology run wild. Technology must be focused by the citizen for the benefit of the citizen; it should seek to secure universal human rights and provide shelter, water, food, health, education, hope and freedom for all. It is my belief that the sustainable city could provide the framework for the fulfilment of these basic human rights. That ideal underpins my approach to sustainability: mobilising creative thinking and technology to secure humanity's future on this small planet of finite resources. It is an innovation that would have an impact on the city of the twenty-first century as radical as that of the industrial revolution on the city of the nineteenth century.

2   Sustainable cities

The planet is not inanimate. It is a living organism. The earth, its rocks, oceans, atmosphere and all living things are one great organism. A coherent holistic system of life, self-regulating, self-changing.

James Lovelock,
GAIA principle

2

Cities have never contained so many, nor so large a proportion of the human race. Between 1950 and 1990 the population of the world's cities increased ten-fold, soaring from 200 million to more than 2 billion. The future of civilisation will be determined by its cities and in its cities.

Today's cities are consuming three-quarters of the world's energy and causing at least three-quarters of global pollution. They are the place of production and consumption of most industrial goods. Cities have become parasites on the landscape – huge organisms draining the world for their sustenance and energy: relentless consumers, relentless polluters.

If the developed world considers its problems of pollution, congestion and inner-city decay are appalling, then consider the changes that are overwhelming the developing world. While in the developed world city populations are effectively stagnating, in the developing world the multiple pressures of urban population explosion, economic development and migration from the countryside are expanding cities at a terrifying rate. In 1990 there were 35 cities with populations over 5 million, 22 of them in the developing world. By the year 2000, it is estimated that there will be 57 cities over the 5-million mark, of which 44 will be in the developing world.

▲ *previous page*
The Endless City

Mexico City's population has grown from 100,000 to 20 million in less than a hundred years. Sprawling, filthy, dangerous but still a centre of glamour, wealth, dreams and hope. People continue to pour in from the countryside at the rate of 80,000 per month.
Stuart Franklin – Magnum/ National Geographical Society image Collection

Over the next thirty years, a further 2 billion people are expected to be added to the cities of the developing world. This massive urbanisation will cause an exponential growth in the volume of resources consumed and of pollution created. Yet perversely, at least half of this growing urban population will be living in shanty towns with no running water, no electricity, no sanitation, and little hope. At least 600 million people already live in life-threatening urban environments. Our multiplying cities threaten overwhelming pollution, and a global society polarised into the haves and have-nots.

Mexico City exemplifies this twin threat: it has the dubious distinction of being the largest and most polluted city in the world. Its population in 1900 was 340,000; it is now home to over 20 million people and 4 million cars, and it is the industrial heartland of Mexico. Visitors arriving by plane often think that they are flying into a rainstorm – which is, in fact, a layer of smog four times worse than that over Los Angeles and six times more toxic than the acceptable standard set by the World Health Organisation (WHO). The ozone count exceeds the danger level for more than 300 days a year; when pollution is too intense, industrial production is halted and the public are urged to stay indoors. And yet rural emigration continues. In 1996 Mexico City faced the logistical problem of providing housing, public utilities and services for 70,000 extra residents a month. Given the impossible constraints, Mexico City, like so many other rapidly expanding cities, is failing to grow sustainably.

This chapter focuses on how cities could be designed to absorb massive increases in urban growth and be sustainable: cities that offer opportunity today without jeopardising future generations.

As long ago as 1966, the economist Kenneth Boulding argued that we must cease to behave as if we lived in a 'cowboy economy' with unlimited new territory to be conquered and resources to be consumed. Instead we must begin to think of our planet as a 'spaceship' – a closed system with finite resources. In fact life on earth is entirely derived from a closed system into which nothing enters except energy from the sun. The sun through photosynthesis gives life to vegetation and creates oxygen. Over thousands of millennia, decaying vegetation forms stocks of solar energy: fossil fuels like coal and oil. The release of these stocks of solar energy through their consumption causes a cocktail of pollution that creates acid rain and that is deemed by many to produce global warming. But the sun is the daily replenishing energy source that creates wind and

Tapping into renewable energies

▲ Harvesting solar energy, Odeille, France.
Leonard Freed – Magnum

▲ Harvesting wind power. Tarifac, Spain.
Bruno Barbey – Magnum

▶ Wind, waves and vegetation: the planet is not inanimate. It is a living organism . . . every element of the planet's biosphere is a constantly renewed resource.

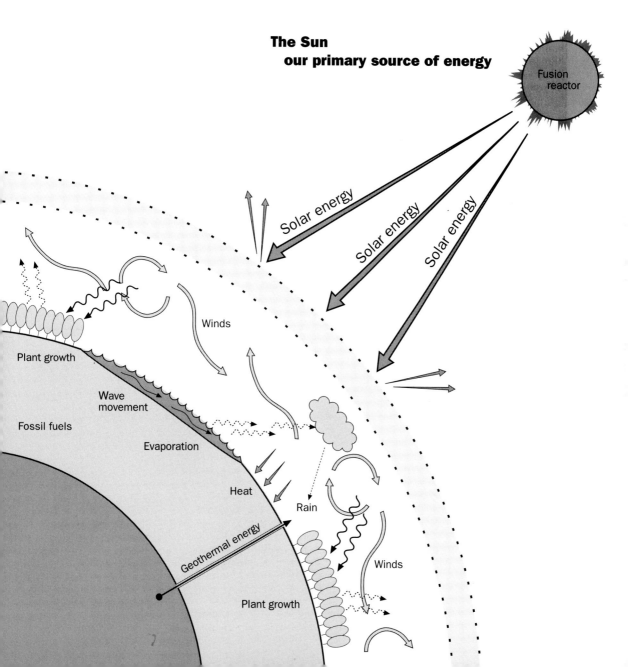

rain, and these constantly 'renewed' energies can be harvested and consumed without polluting the environment.

Cities themselves must be viewed as ecological systems and this attitude must inform our approach to designing cities and managing their use of resources. The resources devoured by a city may be measured in terms of its 'ecological footprint' – an area, scattered throughout the world and vastly greater than the physical boundary of the city itself, on which a city depends. These footprints supply the cities' resources and provide sites for the disposal of their waste and pollution. The ecological footprints of existing cities already virtually cover the entire globe. As the new consumerist cities expand so competition for these resource footprints grow. The expansion of urban ecological footprints is taking place simultaneously with the erosion of fertile lands, living seas and virgin rain forests. Given this simple supply constraint, urban ecological footprints must be dramatically reduced and circumscribed.

The urban ecologist Herbert Girardet has argued that the key lies in cities aiming at a circular 'metabolism', where consumption is reduced by implementing efficiencies and where re-use of resources is maximised. We must recycle materials, reduce waste, conserve exhaustible energies and tap into renewable ones. Since the large majority of production and consumption takes place in cities, current linear processes that create pollution from production must be replaced by those that aim at a circular system of use and re-use. These processes increase a city's overall efficiency and reduce its impact on the environment. To achieve this, we must plan our cities to manage their use of resources, and to do this we need to develop a new form of comprehensive holistic urban planning.

The city is a complex and changing matrix of human activities and environmental effects. To plan for a sustainable city requires the

Linear metabolism cities consume and pollute at a high rate

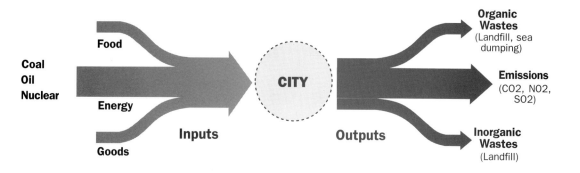

Coal
Oil
Nuclear

Food

Energy

Goods

Inputs

CITY

Outputs

Organic Wastes
(Landfill, sea dumping)

Emissions
(CO2, NO2, SO2)

Inorganic Wastes
(Landfill)

Circular metabolism cities minimise new inputs and maximise recycling

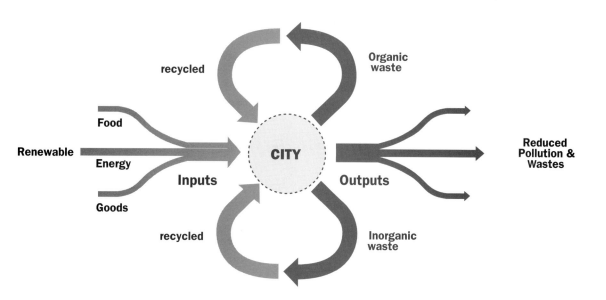

Renewable

Food

Energy

Goods

Inputs

recycled

recycled

CITY

Outputs

Organic waste

Inorganic waste

Reduced Pollution & Wastes

broadest understanding of the relationships between citizens, services, transport policies and energy generation, as well as of their total impact on the local environment and the larger geographic sphere. If a city is to create real sustainability then all these factors must be intertwined. There will be no environmentally sustainable cities until urban ecology, economics and sociology are factored into city planning. The achievement of this goal depends on motivating citizens. Tackling the global environmental crisis from the vantage point of each city brings the task within the grasp of the citizen.

Environmental issues are not distinct from social ones. Policies aimed at improving the environment can also improve the social life of citizens. Ecological and social solutions reinforce each other and build healthier, livelier, more open-minded cities. Above all, sustainability means a good life for future generations.

My own approach to urban sustainability reinterprets and reinvents the 'dense city' model. It is worth remembering why, in this century, this model was so categorically rejected. The industrial cities of the nineteenth century were hell: they suffered extremes of overcrowding, poverty and ill-health. Stinking open sewers spread cholera and typhoid; toxic industries stood side by side with overflowing tenements. As a result, life expectancy in many of the industrial cities of Victorian England was less than twenty-five years. It was precisely these hazards and basic inequities that led planners like Ebenezer Howard in 1898, and Patrick Abercrombie in 1944, to propose decanting populations into less dense and greener surroundings: Garden Cities and New Towns.

Today, by contrast, dirty industry is disappearing from cities of the developed world. In theory at least, with the availability of 'green' manufacturing, virtually clean power generation and public transport systems, and advanced sewerage and waste systems, the dense city model need not be seen as a health hazard. This means we can reconsider the social advantages of proximity, rediscover the advantages of living in each other's company.

Beyond social opportunity the 'dense city' model can bring major ecological benefits. Dense cities can through integrated planning be designed to increase energy efficiency, consume fewer resources, produce less pollution and avoid sprawling over the countryside. It is for these reasons that I believe we should be investing in the idea of a 'Compact City' – a dense and socially diverse city where economic and social activities overlap and where communities are focused around neighbourhoods.

This concept differs radically from today's dominant urban model, that of the United States: a city zoned by function with downtown office areas, out-of-town shopping and leisure centres, residential suburbs and highways. So powerful is this image and so prevalent are the forces that motivate its creation (set by the market-driven criteria of commercial developers) that the less developed countries are now locked into a trajectory that has already failed the developed countries.

The pursuit of this approach is having quantifiably disastrous results. The reason for its continued adoption is economic expediency. If the compact and overlapping approach embraces complexity, the zoned approach rejects it, reducing the city to simplistic divisions and easily managed legal and economic packages. Even at the scale of individual buildings, developers both public and private are turning their backs on the concept of mixed use. Traditional city buildings, in which studios sit over family homes, which sit over offices, which sit over shops, bring life to the street and reduce the need for citizens to get into their cars to meet everyday needs. But these mixed-use buildings create complex tenancies which local authorities find hard

to manage and developers find hard to finance and sell. Instead, public and private developers prefer single-function buildings. And when embarking on major projects they prefer large open sites or cheap 'green-field' ones which offer the possibility of constructing whole housing estates or business parks with minimal leasehold complications. Furthermore, these sites facilitate maximum standardisation of design and construction, thus furthering cost-effectiveness and the argument against mixed-use. The search for short-term profit and quick results continues to turn investment away from complex mixed-use urban development and its inherent social and environmental benefits.

But it is the car which has played the critical role in undermining the cohesive social structure of the city. There are an estimated 500 million cars in the world today. They have eroded the quality of public spaces and have encouraged suburban sprawl. Just as the elevator made the skyscraper possible, so the car has enabled citizens to live away from city centres. The car has made viable the whole concept of dividing everyday activities into compartments, segregating offices, shops and homes. And the wider cities spread out, the more uneconomic it becomes to expand their public transport systems, and the more car-dependent citizens become. Cities around the world are being transformed to facilitate the car even though it is cars rather than industry that are now generating the largest amount of air pollution, the very same pollution that the suburban dwellers are fleeing. In all, 2 trillion cubic metres of exhaust fumes per year are created, and the number of cars is likely to rise by 50 per cent by 2010 and to double by 2030. Paradoxically, from the perspective of the individual, the car remains the century's most liberating and most desired technological product. It is cheap because it is manufactured in volume and is subsidised; it is practical because cities have not been planned to rely on public transport; and it is an irresistible cultural icon that delivers glamour and status.

Cars, cars, cars

By the middle of the twentieth century, there were 2.6 billion people on earth and 50 million cars. In the last fifty years the global population has doubled while the number of cars has increased tenfold. In the next twenty-five years the world population of cars is expected to reach a billion. Mass motorisation has arrived and is set to spread to every city in the world.

◀ Traffic in the centre of Buenos Aires, Argentina.
Morgan – Greenpeace

Simple logistics show how damage is caused by increasing car ownership. First the street, once the local playground and general meeting place, is taken over by parked cars. An efficient parking standard requires 20 square metres for a single car. Even supposing that only one in five inhabitants owns a car, then, a city of 10 million (roughly that of London) needs an area about ten times the size of the City of London ('the square mile'), just to park cars. But start up those 2 million cars and drive off, and you saturate the city with pollution and congestion that harass and divide communities. As transport by car becomes integral to city planning, the street corners and the shapes and surfaces of public spaces are all determined for the benefit of the motorist. Eventually the entire city, from its overall shape and spacing of new buildings to the design of its curbs, lamp posts and railings, is designed according to this one criterion.

Car ownership more than doubled in Europe between 1970 and 1995, and is about to soar in developing cities. It continues to be encouraged by those supporting both nationalised and privatised car industries. And the anticipation of astronomically high levels of car use in the future has led planners to design cities around road specifications, effectively encouraging ever-increasing car use.

Research in San Francisco has compared streets in different neighbourhoods to evaluate the impact of road traffic on the sense of local community. The movement of individuals between houses in busy and quiet streets was monitored in different neighbourhoods. The data reveals the shocking but predictable reality that the level of social interaction between neighbours in a given street, the sense of community in that street, is inversely related to the amount of traffic passing through. This study points the finger at urban traffic as a fundamental cause for the alienation of the urban resident, an effect at the heart of the erosion of modern-day citizenship.

Friends or traffic?

▶ Pedestrian traffic flows.

Research in San Francisco confirms the simple reality that urban traffic undermines a street's sense of community.

In a single neighbourhood three streets with different intensities of traffic are compared. As traffic increases so casual visits to neighbours decline.

Traffic is a significant cause of urban alienation.

Light Traffic

   3.0 friends per person
   6.3 acquaintances

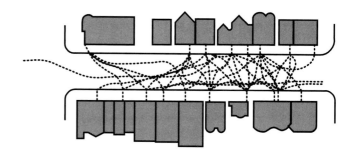

Moderate Traffic

   1.3 friends per person
   4.1 acquaintances

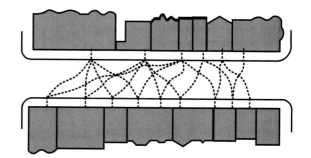

Heavy Traffic

   0.9 friends per person
   3.1 acquaintances

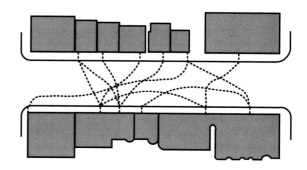

Fortunately, the hidden cost of the zoned urban model is finally being recognised. In the United States the economic cost of traffic congestion, in terms of squandered energy and lost time, is about $150 billion per year, equivalent to the gross national product of Denmark. And this figure does not begin to address the social costs including health, recently estimated by the World Resources Institute (WRI) as a further $300 billion. Both figures exclude damage to the natural environment and, crucially, the social cost of isolation and disenfranchisement of those citizens left scratching a living in isolated and rotting city ghettos, while the city empties itself out into ever more exclusive suburbs. The *New York Times* recently headlined the dramatic problems of gridlock and pollution engendered by the sprawling 'paradise' cities of Phoenix, Denver, Las Vegas and Salt Lake City. Phoenix is now larger than Los Angeles with only a third of its population. Its quality of air ranks among the country's worst outside Southern California.

The creation of the modern Compact City demands the rejection of single-function development and the dominance of the car. The question is how to design cities in which communities thrive and mobility is increased – how to design for personal mobility without allowing the car to undermine communal life, how to design for and accelerate the use of clean transport systems and re-balance the use of our streets in favour of the pedestrian and the community.

The Compact City addresses these issues. It grows around centres of social and commercial activity located at public transport nodes. These provide the focal points around which neighbourhoods develop. The Compact City is a network of these neighbourhoods, each with its own parks and public spaces and accommodating a diversity of overlapping private and public activities. London's historic structure of towns, villages, squares and parks is typical of a polycentric pattern of development. Most importantly, these

Compact mixed-use nodes reduce journey requirements and create lively sustainable neighbourhoods

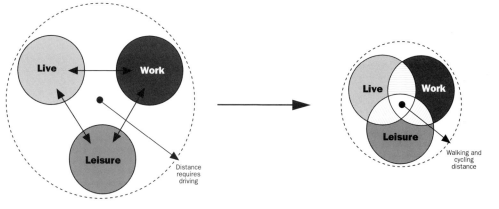

Zoning of activities leads to reliance on the private car.

Compact nodes reduce travel and allow walking and cycling.

Compact nodes linked by mass-transit systems can be arranged in response to local constraints

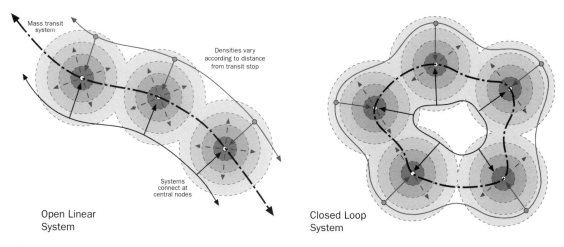

Open Linear System

Closed Loop System

neighbourhoods bring work and facilities within convenient reach of the community, and this proximity means less driving for everyday needs. In large cities, Mass Transit Systems can provide high-speed cross-town travel by linking one neighbourhood centre with another, leaving local distribution to local systems. This reduces the volume and impact of through traffic, which can be calmed and controlled, particularly around the public heart of neighbourhoods. Local trams, light railway systems and electric buses become more effective, and cycling and walking more pleasant. Congestion and pollution in the streets are drastically reduced and the sense of security and conviviality of public space is increased.

Sustainable Compact Cities could, I contend, reinstate the city as the ideal habitat for a community-based society. It is an established type of urban structure that can be interpreted in all manner of ways in response to all manner of cultures. Cities should be about the people they shelter, about face-to-face contact, about condensing the ferment of human activity, about generating and expressing local culture. Whether in a temperate or an extreme climate, in a rich or poor society, the long-term aim of sustainable development is to create a flexible structure for a vigorous community within a healthy and non-polluting environment.

Proximity, the provision of good public space, the presence of natural landscape and the exploitation of new urban technologies can radically improve the quality of air and of life in the dense city. Another benefit of compactness is that the countryside itself is protected from the encroachment of urban development. I will show how the concentration of diverse activities, rather than the grouping of similar activities, can make for more efficient use of energy. The Compact City can provide an environment as beautiful as that of the countryside.

In 1991 the Mayor of Shanghai invited my practice to propose a strategic framework for a new district of his city. This offered us the chance to explore and apply the principles of the sustainable Compact City.

The context of the commission is revealing. China has 1.5 billion people and makes up about one quarter of the world's population. Their nation is undergoing the largest migration in its history from country to city, a journey that has seen at least 80 million people moving into shanties around China's main cities in less than a generation. Traditionally, the Chinese viewed cities and their agricultural hinterland as a totality. Even today, the Shanghai metropolitan area is nearly self-sufficient in vegetables and grain. But in the rush to industrialise and urbanise, the ecology has suffered. Of the ten cities suffering the worst air pollution in the world, five are in China. Four of China's seven most important river systems are contaminated, and acid rain affects almost a third of China's territory. Cities like Shenzhen, Dongguan and Zhuhai are flattening colossal tracts of countryside either to supply construction materials or to pave the way for future development. Cities like Shenzhen have grown from 100,000 to 3 million in 15 years. Urbanisation is the first phase in the transformation of a communal rural society into a consumerist urban one. China's new cities are planned around motorways rather than public transport. Ownership of cars is therefore expected to grow from 1.8 million today to reach 20 million by 2010. As the populations of the new cities swell, a process of industrialisation will follow to provide the classic menu of consumerist goods, guaranteeing the huge economic growth that is the basis of the Chinese economic 'miracle'.

In 1990 Shanghai, the world's fifth largest city, had a population of 13 million. In five years it is planned to have more than 17 million. Shanghai's ambition is to consolidate its status as the commercial

China's urban miracle?

▲ View of the Pudong from old Shanghai.
G. Pinkhassov – Magnum

▶ Shenzhen has grown from 100,000 to 3 million in fifteen years; China is encouraging the migration of millions of its rural population to fill the new cities.
Donovan Wylie – Magnum

hub of China and a major force in world finance. Sadly, the city intends to follow the old Western model and motorise its existing 7 million cyclists. Shanghai is a stunning city, dense and teeming with life. Early twentieth-century office blocks edge the famous tree-lined riverside of the Bund – a waterfront which combines the elegance of the Promenade des Anglais in Nice with the power of Liverpool's great Merseyside frontage. But the Bund has been the first casualty in Shanghai's drive to convert to the car. Its majestic lines of trees have been felled to make way for a continuous riverside car park and elevated promenade that blocks the magnificent views of the river from the city.

The river itself, the Huangpo, is almost a kilometre wide and is criss-crossed by merchant shipping of every shape and size. Across the river lies the Pudong, a vast development area covering thousands of hectares; and in the part of the Pudong which is immediately opposite the heart of old Shanghai lies the site of the new district – the Lu Zia Sui, a teardrop-shaped area one and a half kilometres square and remarkably similar in form to London's Isle of Dogs. It is here that the Pudong has recently been linked to Shanghai by two of the world's longest single-span bridges, as well as by a network of tunnels. Intended purely as an office development for half a million workers, the Lu Zia Sui project was seen as a Canary Wharf-type development but many times larger.

Although Shanghai has a rich urban culture of its own, the scheme proposed by the Shanghai authorities turned its back on the cultural and commercial diversity of the old city. Instead, the new district was to be purely for international office users, and designed primarily to be accessed by car. Traffic engineers planned for the predicted huge rush-hour traffic by designing massive road systems – sometimes double- and triple-decked – and a counter-network of pedestrian underpasses and footbridges. Road coverage on the site was three

Let's motor

▲ Shanghai aims to motorise 7 million cyclists by the year 2000.
Michael K. Nichols – Magnum

times greater than in New York, but with less than half New York's building density. In all, barely one third of the site was left for buildings. As each building plot was isolated by highways, the proposals would have resulted in a district of stand-alone individual blocks and towers surrounded by a sea of cars – for some the ultimate image of progress in the shape of the modern international city.

In contrast, our approach sought to avoid creating a private financial ghetto detached from the life of the city. Instead, we promoted the idea of Lu Zia Sui as a diverse commercial and residential quarter enhanced by a network of parks and public spaces and accessed primarily by public transport, an area capable of acting as a cultural focus for the whole Pudong. This approach would also safeguard the district against the boom–bust cycle of the international office market, which so notoriously bankrupted single-function developments such as Canary Wharf in London. Above all, we aimed to establish sustainable local communities, convivial neighbourhoods that would also consume only half the energy of their conventionally planned counterparts, and would limit their impact on the environment.

Our transport and environmental engineers Ove Arup and Partners calculated that our broader mix of activities and greater emphasis on public transport could reduce the need for car journeys and thus roads by as much as 60 per cent. The balance between single-use road space and multi-use public space could be altered in favour of the latter. We vastly expanded the network of pedestrian-biased streets, cycle paths, market places and avenues, and made room for a substantial park. This network of public spaces sought to enable the 'open-minded' cultural activities of the city. It was carefully interwoven with the public transport system to make a single, interconnected web of public space and movement that started at

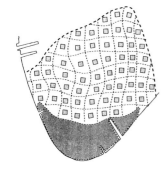

Lu Zia Sui – before

▲ Slavish adherence to conventional market and transportation criteria had determined the form of the new area – a grid of individual stand alone buildings ringed by heavily congested streets.

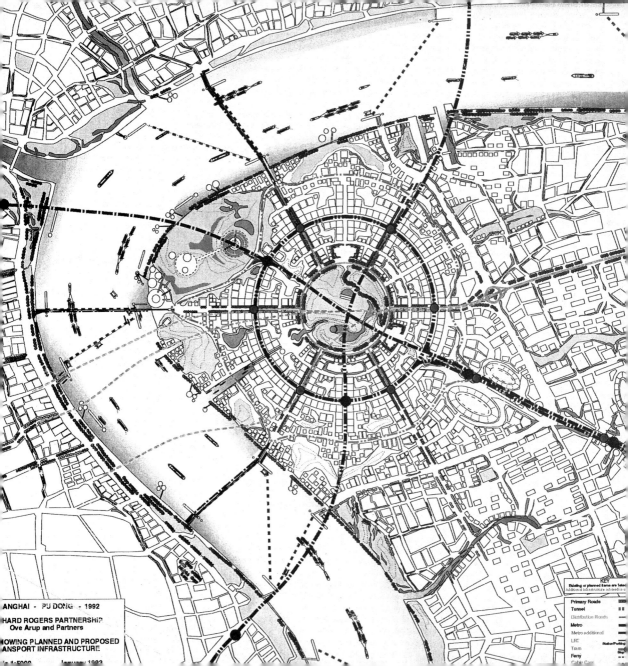

SHANGHAI - PU DONG - 1992

RICHARD ROGERS PARTNERSHIP
Ove Arup and Partners

SHOWING PLANNED AND PROPOSED
TRANSPORT INFRASTRUCTURE

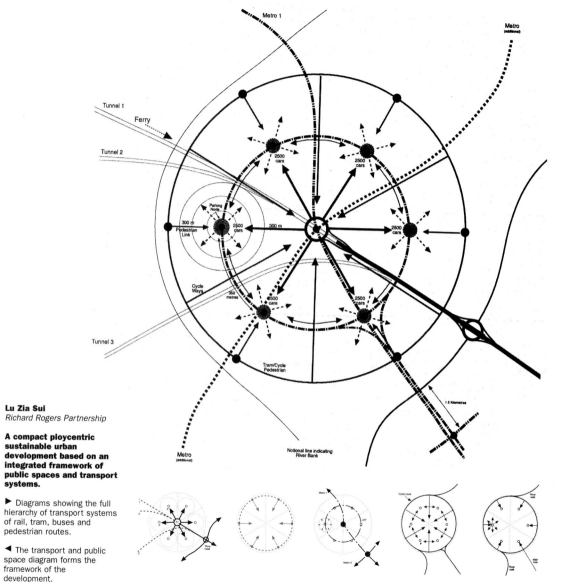

Metro 1

Metro
(additional)

Tunnel 1

Ferry

Tunnel 2

2500
cars

2500
cars

Parking
Node

300 m
Pedestrian
Link

300 m

2500
cars

2500
cars

Cycle
Ways

350
metres

2500
cars

2500
cars

Tunnel 3

Tram/Cycle
Pedestrian

1.5 Kilometres

Lu Zia Sui
Richard Rogers Partnership

A compact ploycentric sustainable urban development based on an integrated framework of public spaces and transport systems.

▶ Diagrams showing the full hierarchy of transport systems of rail, tram, buses and pedestrian routes.

◀ The transport and public space diagram forms the framework of the development.

Metro
(additional)

Notional line indicating
River Bank

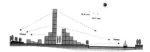

Lu Zia Sui
Richard Rogers Partnership

▲ The profile of the new city is set by general guidelines that maximise daylight penetration to streets and buildings and use prevailing winds to help cool and freshen air.

◀ First model showing the main principles of the urban framework. The six mixed use communities spatially define a common central urban park. Buildings of varying heights are grouped so that their impact on other buildings and public spaces is reduced.

the citizen's front door and led ultimately, via car parks, buses and trams, to stations and airports. A flexible hierarchy of different modes of transport, ranging from safe sidewalks to high-speed trains and planes, afforded seamless mobility for all citizens.

At the heart of the Lu Zia Sui was the central park, from which radiating boulevards linked three concentric avenues. The outer avenue carried pedestrians and cyclists only; the second, trams and buses; and the inner, partially sunken, the main car routes. The overall aim was to locate the community's everyday needs, including public transport, within comfortable walking distance and away from through traffic.

Six large compact neighbourhoods of 80,000 people each were focused around each of the main transport interchanges and connected to the main public domain network. Each neighbourhood had its own distinct character, and all lay within ten minutes' walk of the central park, the river and adjacent neighbourhoods. Offices, commercial premises, shops and cultural institutions were concentrated closer to the busy metropolitan underground stations, while residential buildings were mainly clustered around the park and by the river, together with hospitals, schools and other community-based buildings.

With fewer roads and isolated sites, buildings could be joined together to form streets and squares. By varying the heights of buildings, sunlight and daylight could be focused on enlivening the streets, squares and avenues, even though density of construction was high. The variety of roofline also optimised views and the penetration of daylight into the buildings themselves, reducing the need for energy for artificial lighting. The overall composition produced a dense city profile crowned by a series of towers – a striking skyline across the river from old Shanghai.

The whole premise of the Compact City is that interventions trigger further opportunities for efficiency. A Compact City composed of overlapping activities, for instance, is more convivial and can reduce the need for car journeys, which in turn dramatically reduces the energy used for transportation – usually a quarter of a city's overall energy consumption. Fewer cars mean less congestion and better air quality, which in turn encourages cycling and walking rather than driving. Better air quality makes opening windows to fresh air more attractive than turning on filtered air-conditioners.

There are other important environmental advantages to a compact form of city that has fewer roads but more landscaped public spaces. Parks, gardens, trees and other landscaping provide vegetation that shades and cools streets, courtyards and buildings in summer. Cities are generally 1–2°C warmer than their hinterland. The overall effect of rich urban landscaping is to reduce the heat 'bloom' of cities, measurably reducing the need for air-conditioning. Plants dampen noise levels and filter pollution, absorb carbon dioxide and produce oxygen – further factors that reduce the need for air-conditioning to supply cooled fresh air to buildings in what would otherwise be hot and polluted urban areas. Urban landscape absorbs rain, reducing the discharge of urban rainfall and storm water. Landscape plays an important psychological role in the city and can sustain a wide diversity of urban wildlife.

Certain North American cities have achieved 70 per cent efficiency in recycling city waste. This compares with Copenhagen at 55 per cent and London at 5 per cent. City waste should be seen as a resource to be mined.

A Compact City reduces the waste of energy. Generating electric power produces hot water as a by-product, which in conventional power plants is simply wasted. Local Combined Heat and Power plants (CHPs) can be used both to distribute electricity and, due to their proximity, to pipe hot water directly into buildings. This can more than double the efficiency of conventional urban power distribution. City rubbish, which is usually either dumped as landfill or incinerated, both with polluting effects, can be burned by local

The conventional system - remote power generation

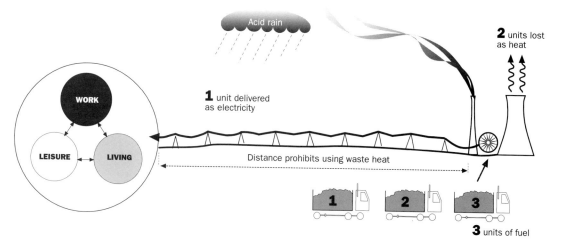

Acid rain

2 units lost as heat

1 unit delivered as electricity

WORK

LEISURE ↔ LIVING

Distance prohibits using waste heat

1 **2** **3**

3 units of fuel

The compact model - local power generation and waste recycling

WORK

LEISURE LIVING

Compact mixed use development allows energy to be shared between activities

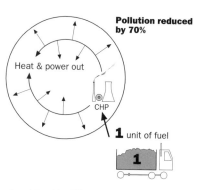

Pollution reduced by 70%

Heat & power out

CHP

1 unit of fuel

1

Local Combined Heat and Power stations (CHP's) are twice as effective because they distrubute electricity and heat

Clean Waste in

CHP

2/3 unit

2/3

Local waste can be burnt in CHP's further reducing energy input

CHPs and supply up to 30 per cent of a community's energy needs. In a city that combines a variety of activities, it is easier to transfer waste heat from one activity to another. Excess heat generated by offices, for example, is usually dissipated into the environment, but it can be reused in hospitals, homes, hotels or schools if they are reasonably close.

Human waste that is rich in nutrients is currently discharged in such high concentrations that it poisons the environment. It can instead be recycled to produce methane fuel pellets and fertilizers. Grey water can be filtered through natural systems on site and be re-used for irrigation of urban landscape or to restock local aquifers. Experimental sewerage treatment schemes that discharge their waste below industrial forestry have been shown both to increase the growth rate of the forests, woods and parks and to restock local aquifers with purified water. Clean water is recognised as the critical resource of the coming millennium, and we must develop systems that maximise the efficiency of its use.

At the outset of the Shanghai project we targeted a 50 per cent overall reduction of energy use. We were amazed when we later calculated that the 'circular' approach would have meant a 70 per cent saving. In commercial terms this implied a real downsizing of demand requirements for new power stations – good news for the environment – and also a dramatic decrease in the long-term cost of living for businesses and residents.

Sustainable urban planning is made possible by computer modelling that brings together the complex matrix of criteria that make up the modern city. In the Shanghai project, our design team could measure the impact of strategies on energy consumption, transport needs, parking requirements, pedestrian movement and the optimising of sunlight. The computer model was used to adjust the mixture of activities within neighbourhoods to produce the most efficient use of energy around the clock and through the seasons. The model also enabled the public investments likely to be needed for roads, public transport and power infrastructure to be treated as variables, and to be gauged against each other in terms of monetary and environmental cost. Highly articulated computer modelling helped all those involved to co-ordinate activities and to assess the overall implications of every decision. It is also our best tool to communicate the complex issues of urban planning to the city official, the investor and the citizen.

Whether Shanghai will pursue any of these sustainable strategies is open to question. Political and commercial pressures have already led to the sale of isolated sites. Plots have been identified on a grid and the highest building in China is to be erected in the very centre of our unbuilt park. The current building process requires new roads to service the plots already sold, and so the classic market-driven form of unsustainable development will emerge. Unless the government of China shows real resolve and commits itself to planning for sustainable cities, it will soon be faced with massive congestion, pollution and social dissatisfaction on an even larger scale than is endemic to the cities it is using as role models.

The Lu Zia Sui project is not a model to be imposed, but rather a local illustration of an initial approach to planning for sustainable urban development. The distinction is crucial. All settlements, from rural hamlets to the largest metropolis, from those with vast resources to those with precious few, have something to gain from sustainable thinking and planning. Small towns, for example, can make ideal sustainable developments as they offer the possibility of integrating both urban and agricultural strategies. But in every case, building a sustainable city requires a holistic discipline of planning that considers all the factors which make up the physical, social and economic needs of a community and relates them to the greater environment. This type of planning necessitates the comparative analysis of population, energy, water, transport, topography, employment and, most importantly, local technology and culture.

In 1994 we were given the opportunity to test this approach on a small scale when we were commissioned to plan a sustainable 'post-industrial' information-based 'technopolis' for 5000 inhabitants in the hills of Majorca – a settlement based on proximity to knowledge, in this case a university, and located in a quality environment that enjoyed an ideal climate.

Our first step was to resolve the most obvious problem: how to make this new settlement on arid land self-sufficient in water. Our environmental consultants calculated that by collecting 10 per cent of the annual rainfall on the surrounding landscape, we could supply water to the new inhabitants and improve irrigation of local crops. We proposed to structure the community into three linked villages carved into the parched hills. A new distribution network provided domestic water and fed a system of fountains, troughs and ponds which cooled the streets and squares and irrigated the trees and plants. The run-off water and the grey water from the villages were used to irrigate the surrounding farmlands. This improved irrigation to the neighbouring farmland and greatly increased the diversity and volume of crop production – strengthening the viability of the traditional agricultural community itself.

We concentrated on harvesting existing and available sources of renewable energy, including sun through photo-voltaic cells, wind through turbines and crops such as willow, which can be burned in local CHPs to produce power. This boosted agricultural employment, and closed the circle between the production of carbon dioxide when generating power and its absorption by new planting – an efficient use of energy renewed through photosynthesis.

The buildings were laid out so as to make full use of the elements to cool and protect the streets and courtyards – a process of

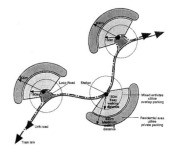

**Majorca Technopolis
First sketches**
Richard Rogers Partnership

▲ The technopolis was divided into three communities of roughly 2000 residents. Each community was planned around walking and cycling distances. A surface public transport system links the hearts of the three communities.

▶ Branch and leaf: the streets radiate from the social centre of each community while the development follows the gentle contours of the site. Tops of hills are left free of buildings.
Eamonn O'Mahony

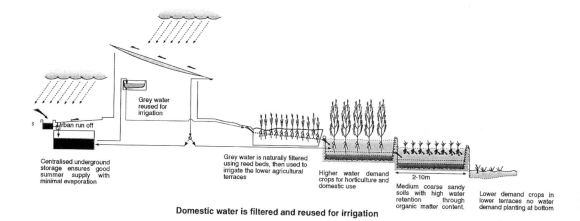

Grey water reused for irrigation

Urban run off

Centralised underground storage ensures good summer supply with minimal evaporation

Grey water is naturally filtered using reed beds, then used to irrigate the lower agricultural terraces

Higher water demand crops for horticulture and domestic use

2-10m

Medium coarse sandy soils with high water retention through organic matter content.

Lower demand crops in lower terraces no water demand planting at bottom

Domestic water is filtered and reused for irrigation

shaping construction to benefit from every environmental condition. The street pattern was laid out to encourage walking and conviviality. The Majorca development sought to make maximum use of all local resources, particularly labour, to create a low-cost, cheap-to-run settlement which could foster a healthy and sociable lifestyle for the community. In many ways, sustainable development at this scale mirrors the process which shaped traditional settlements from desert towns to mountain villages.

The concept of sustainability must also be applied to 'urban renewal' and 're-development' projects. Most cities of the developed world have suffered intense de-industrialisation over the past twenty years, leaving a legacy of vast abandoned sites, often located along the central transportation routes and along rivers, freightways, canals and the sea. Other cities, such as Berlin, Beirut, Saigon, Sarajevo and Grozny, have been devastated by armed conflict. In the case of Berlin and Beirut, the Wall and the Green Line respectively separated the opposing factions and cut the cities in half. As a result, the heaviest destruction was at the very heart of their historic and cultural centres. Whether caused by de-industrialisation or conflict, these redevelopment sites represent important opportunities to improve the sustainability of cities.

In the developing world, by contrast, cities are expanding too rapidly, resulting in the emergence of massive shanty towns. 50 per cent of the world's urban population are new to the city; for many the first and only experience of modern city life is the shanty. In most cities, these settlements (normally illegal) lack even the most rudimentary services such as drainage, electricity and clean water. Alarmingly, political instability, persecution, famine, deforestation and other such pressures continue to drive rural people to the cities even when there is no commercial base to support them. In Bombay 5 million people – roughly equivalent to the entire residential population of

Shanty in Rio de Janeiro, or Bombay, Mexico City, Lagos, Istanbul . . .

Throughout the world rural immigrants to cities cram into open-sewer shanty districts. In Bogota, for example, some 59 per cent of the population live in shanties. Many of these informal settlements establish themselves on unstable or unsafe land and are at the mercy of earthquakes, landslides, disease, droughts and flooding.

▶ Port au Prince. *Jenny Matthews – AVRU/Oxfam*

inner London – live in shanties. It has been estimated that 30 to 60 per cent of the residents of most large cities in developing countries live in 'informal settlements' or shanty towns. The UNCHS Global Report on Human Settlements (1986) states that in São Paulo 32 per cent of the total population live in shanty towns; in Mexico City this proportion is 40 per cent, in Manila 47 per cent and in Bogota 59 per cent. In Argentina these districts are known as *villas miserias*, townships of misery. These settlements tend to be founded on marginal land, such as flood plains or unstable slopes, rendering them vulnerable to natural hazards such as flooding, landslides or earthquakes. They have no public utilities for water, sewerage, rubbish collection and power, and as a consequence their inhabitants suffer from the effects of polluted air, water and streets. They need safe energy sources for cooking and heating that reduce air pollution and the risk of fire, sanitation systems to protect water supplies and reduce disease, drainage systems to reduce flooding and public transport to increase access.

We need to find the technical support and funding for affordable infrastructures to service these areas, and to create partnerships to guide the improvement of their living conditions. It is here that citizenship and participation can reap major rewards. Though only a tiny proportion of the total, there are cases of shanty settlements that have displayed enough social cohesiveness and resourcefulness to transform themselves into viable low-cost towns: laying their own drains, cables and water supplies and prioritising the order in which improvements are implemented. Most importantly, this approach has allowed the individual communities to create the unique living conditions that respond to their particular cultural and economic needs. In the absence of a fairer distribution of wealth, the best way of helping squatter settlements is to encourage self-help by providing technical leadership, low-cost funding and political support.

Examples of sustainable development are appearing in the developing world. Curitiba, a Brazilian city of 1.5 million residents, once suffered from the usual problems of rapid expansion and desperate shanty towns, but has now emerged as leader among sustainable cities. It has made sustainability and citizen participation the guiding principle of its daily life and the environment its top priority. During his terms as Curitiba's mayor, architect Jamie Lerner tackled its problems with broad policies. As the shanty towns were mostly contained on the banks of the city's rivers and lacked formal roads, garbage remained uncollected and became enormous fetid piles on the river banks. The rivers as a consequence were stripped of vegetation and contaminated by raw sewage. Lerner introduced a range of schemes aimed at drawing in the participation of the shanty-dwellers to solve these problems. He offered transport tokens to adults, and books and food to children, in exchange for bags of rubbish delivered to the local dumps. Soon the favelas that had been strewn with festering garbage were cleaned up and landscaped. The mostly unemployed shanty-dwellers are now given opportunities to sell their own crafts and produce in specially built non-corporate shopping centres introduced by the mayor. They can also obtain benefits such as food, rent, education and health care in exchange for their labour. Production and the earnings from labour therefore stay within the community, rather than chasing foreign goods.

Lerner's urban strategies are not limited to addressing the dire problems of the shanty towns, but reach across the whole of Curitiba with a wide spectrum of initiatives. Twenty years ago, Curitiba had half a square metre of open space per citizen. Today, after a systematic programme of landscaping, it has a hundred times more, as well as a network of pedestrian and cycle routes. Lerner has sought to shape the rapid development of the city around its public transport system. The contrast between Curitiba and São Paulo is striking. São Paulo, the third largest and third most polluted city in

Curitiba: promoting urban sustainability

▲ Taking the surface Subway Bus. Each stop is a smart glazed capsule and is manned twenty-four hours a day by the 'conductor'. Passengers buy tickets at the entrance from the conductor who also operates the street to platform lift. The station and buses are designed with multiple entrances similar to an underground train system to minimise loading and unloading times. Taking public transport is safe, swift and smart.
Nani Gois – SMCS

◄ The first university of the environment. As part of Curitiba's holistic approach to planning for sustainability, each school class, including the teacher, spends a week at the university learning how their own small scale interventions contribute to creating real practical benefits for the environment. By encouraging participation, a real cultural ethos is evolved which colours every aspect of life in Curitiba.
Nani Gois – SMCS

the world, is an unbroken mass of buildings punctuated in every direction by high-rise towers; it is constantly gridlocked and pollution levels are dramatic; and the city appears to have no centre, no diversity and no urban coherence.

Lerner's planners have reacted to the pressures of rapid development with a simple strategy. Curitiba is zoned so that its high-rise residential and office buildings line five main axes of public transport: dedicated high-speed and high-capacity surface bus routes built at a cost of $200,000 per kilometre rather than the $60 million per kilometre of a conventional subway system. At the centre of the city the main streets and squares are pedestrianised. The 'Avenue of Flowers' and the 'twenty-four-hour district' contain the civic heart of the Curitiba; all the main public transport systems converge at the centre and obviate the need to drive.

The showpiece of Curitiba and Lerner's vision is the transformation of the city's defunct quarries into a landscaped cultural centre. He has commissioned three financially modest but inspiring cultural projects. One quarry contains the 'university of the environment', built within a circular structure of reclaimed telegraph poles; here, schoolchildren and their teachers follow specific courses explaining the principles and tangible results of urban sustainability. In another, Lerner has commissioned a glazed opera house suspended over a lake, with the dramatic backdrop of the quarry walls. And in a third, he has commissioned a landscaped 25,000-person natural auditorium for concerts and festivals. Curitiba is robust rather than beautiful, but Lerner's urban agenda has created a genuine spirit of participation amongst its citizens. His initiatives have wedded the residents to their city, inspiring an extraordinary amount of pride and providing incentive for further action.

The extraordinary problems of the informal settlements of the urban poor should be tackled from within the community and, as in

Curitiba, those problems must be integrated into the overall urban planning matrix. 'Informal' settlements cannot be planned in an orthodox way, but the process of settlement needs to be encouraged on terrain where the human bearing capacity of the land, in terms of water, energy and resistance to natural disasters, has been proven. Technical support and access to sophisticated topographical and meteorological data can help in the planning of strategic agro-urban systems to deliver safe water, safe energy and food, and in the creation of settlement patterns robust enough to resist predictable environmental hazards. This technology and expertise is being developed primarily in the industrialised world and should be made available as a service to poorer communities.

In South Africa, former Yugoslavia and Chechenia and others where the consolidation of communities is now a political priority, the question of how to build new settlements, and in what form, is crucial. Involving communities in the process of creating healthy, cost-effective, sustainable settlements that respond to local needs and cultures will generate real long-term solutions. Genuine participation is the key to producing urban solutions that can transform lives.

I am convinced that the multitude of proven approaches to building sustainable communities can redress the folly and ignorance of current city building. The commercial and political forces needlessly driving the decline of the environment and the erosion of city life must be tempered by environmentally sustainable and socially equitable urban objectives. To do this, society will need to exploit modern technology and communications, involve its citizens and grapple with the dynamic complexity of the modern city. It will also need to be convinced of the value of civic beauty and pride. In place of cities that overwhelm the environment and alienate our communities, we must build cities that nurture both.

Sustainability requires education for all

◀ Although most of Santa Fe's children have access to primary education, at least a third of them drop out within three years to start work and boost their families' incomes. Only one in a hundred children goes on to higher education.
Stuart Franklin – Magnum

3   Sustainable architecture

When the union of the born and the
made is complete, our fabrications
will learn, adapt, heal themselves and
evolve. This is a power we have
hardly dreamt of yet.

Kevin Kelly,
Out of Control

3　Architecture emerged from mankind's need for shelter. It soon became a fundamental expression of technological skill and of spiritual and social objectives. The history of architecture documents humanity's ingenuity, its sense of harmony and values; it is a profound reflection of the complex motives of individuals and societies.

Architecture extracts beauty from the application of rational thinking. Architecture is the play between knowledge and intuition, logic and the spirit, the measurable and the unmeasurable. As in a Bach fugue, Mondrian's *New York Boogy Woogie* or Becket's *'Waiting for Godot'*, beauty is fused throughout with order. Architecture has a larger measure of function but the aesthetic order is no less essential. The Parthenon, the Tempieto by Bramante or the Salk Centre by Kahn – all reach the sublime through the rational.

Today, the rich complexity of human motivation that generated architecture is being stripped bare. Building is pursued almost exclusively for profit. New buildings are perceived as little more than financial commodities, entries in company balance-sheets. The search for profit determines their form, quality and performance. Any expenditure not directly related to the making of short-term profit exposes developers to longer-term capital outlay, which makes the company less competitive and hence more vulnerable to financial exposure and ultimately to take-over. Our 'bottom-line' economics – whose purpose is startlingly described by the Thatcherite entrepreneur Lord Hanson as 'getting hold of tomorrow's money today' – offer no incentive to invest in ecological technologies that will pay off only in the long term. This strategy, which can only leave tomorrow worse off, is the antithesis of sustainable thinking and completely overrules the aesthetic considerations essential to good architecture: it provides no incentive for such public gestures as an arcade, no reason to use good materials, to landscape a building or even plant a tree.

▲ *previous page*
Woven into nature

Adobe dwelling, Masa Verde,
New Mexico
Mike Davies

The pioneers of the modern movement – Frank Lloyd Wright, Le Corbusier, Mies Van der Rohe, Nervi, Alvar Aalto, Buckminster Fuller, Lubetkin, Prouvé – turned to industrial techniques and new forms because they offered creative freedom and the prospect of social improvements. Today the enormous potential of these techniques is applied to a single end: making money. Look closely at an average commercial development and you will see just how pared-down and crude it is. After a century of refinement, the steel or concrete building has never been so cheap to build, nor built so cheaply. These barren structures, with their classical, neo-vernacular or modern façades chosen as if from catalogues, have no allegiance to place nor people. Buildings of all types are packaged and standardised; architects are selected for their low fees rather than for the quality of their work. The profession is condemned to turning out the largest enclosure for the least money in the shortest time and to dressing its façades in one 'bolt-on' style or another. These buildings are the energy-guzzling structures that are consuming half of the world's annual energy.

But buildings are not merely commodities. They form the backdrop of our lives in the city. Architecture is the art form to which we are continually exposed. It enhances or hinders our lives because it creates the environment in which all our everyday experiences take place, be they commonplace or seminal. There should be no surprise that architecture becomes controversial, nor that it is the art form which the public criticises the most widely and the most passionately. The special status that architecture holds in our lives demands special vigilance from the citizen, and this requires society to be both informed and prescriptive about quality.

The profession too must define an ethical stance. The requirement for architecture to contribute to social and environmental sustainability now charges architects with responsibilities that go

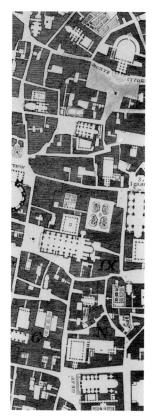

Public and Private

▲ *Giambattista Nolli: Map of Rome 1768*
The city as meeting place. Nolli's plan shows the extensive network of public routes and spaces carved out of the solid of the city: the public realm. A place where citizens interact and where the character of the city is defined both spatially and culturally.

beyond the limits of an autonomous brief. The status and power of the profession has declined under the weight of commercial pressure. Ellen Posner have commented on the dilemma in which the profession finds itself:

As members of a profession currently without an ethic, they have not been driving the discussion. Commissioned by clients to install barrier walls and private pathways that can keep out or discourage those who are unwanted or hired to create private commercial experiences out of what may have been public space, many become complicit in structuring the urban language of separation.

In this chapter I will explore the ways in which buildings can enrich the public space of our cities, respond to the changing needs of their users and exploit technologies that sustain rather than pollute. Buildings should inspire, and compose cities that celebrate society and respect nature. Our present need for sustainable building now offers opportunities to re-establish ambition and to evolve new aesthetic orders – it could provide the impetus for the revival of the profession of architecture.

Cities are a compromise between private rights and public responsibilities. In 1768, the architect Nolli drew a map of Rome; by blacking out the spaces that were private, he illustrated all those that were accessible to the citizen. As well as the passages, streets, squares and parks that we all think of as public, he also included the various semi-public spaces: churches, public baths, town halls and markets. Nolli showed in two dimensions the spaces through which the citizen could pass freely. But it is the three-dimensional mass of each individual building that defines the public realm, a seamless and constantly changing sequence of spaces – the city's signature. We feel this in the compressed spaces of walled cities, where we are led through narrow alleys, then streets, eventually to emerge into the

New York

▲ Central Park
Buildings define the shape
and quality of the public
realm – the city's signature.

drama of an expansive civic place; or in more open cities like Bath, whose circuses, crescents and squares define more pure and generous geometric volumes. Even across the grid of New York, there is a chequerboard pattern of interconnected public spaces, from the 'vest-pocket' Paley Park to Rockefeller Plaza and the magnificent Central Park.

Most of our public parks, squares and avenues are bequeathed to us from previous centuries. In this modern age of democracy one would expect many more important additions to the public realm, but in fact our contribution appears to be the erosion of these spaces by traffic and personal greed. The public realm is being restricted by the overbearing presence of security, the imposition of entrance fees to cultural institutions, the decline of public amenities and the dominance of the car, which reduces public spaces to narrow pavements. And buildings are being designed as if they were stand-alone objects, rather than elements that enclose and shape the public realm.

Buildings enhance the public sphere in a variety of ways: they model the skyline, landmark the city, lead the eye to explore, celebrate the crossing of streets. But even at the most modest level, the way that the building's details (its paving, handrails, kerbs, sculpture, street furniture or signage) relate to the human scale or to the touch has an important impact on the streetscape. The smallest detail has a crucial effect on the totality. A building with any claim to beauty – with any claim, that is, to transcend the everyday and lift the spirit of those who use it – must address these concerns.

Let me give some examples to illustrate how the public realm can inform the shape and concept of a building. In 1984, we entered (and lost) the competition to design an extension to the National Gallery in London. We began by extending our survey well beyond the designated site, which had lain derelict since the war. To our surprise, we found that

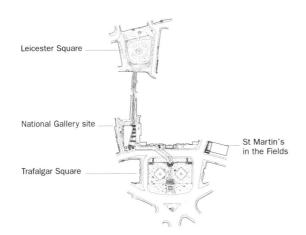

Leicester Square

National Gallery site

Trafalgar Square

St Martin's
in the Fields

◀ The small site sits between two important public places: Trafalgar and Leicester Squares. Conceiving the site as a hinge between the two squares requires a building form that allows both a strong visual and physical connection. The public route became an important defining element of the final design.

◀ The view towards Nelson's Column from beneath the four-storey-high undercroft of the proposed Gallery extension.
John Donat

◀ The proposed 'viewing tower' signals the new public route to Leicester Square and balances the relationship of towers around the main entrance to the National Gallery.
John Donat

this small site held the key to unlocking the isolation of Trafalgar Square – once the heart of the Empire, now a polluted tourist trap encircled by traffic. Isolated from the everyday public life of the city, it is only on the rare occasions when it hosts rallies, demonstrations or celebrations that it regains its civic role. We proposed to reintegrate it by creating a pedestrian route from Trafalgar Square to Leicester Square, through the site of the gallery extension.

The linking of the two squares became the driving concept of the project. We proposed an open flight of public stairs that descended from Leicester Square, passing through our National Gallery extension (taking up almost half of the ground floor) and connecting to Trafalgar Square through a generous galleria beneath the busy roadway. To mark this new route and signal the public entrance of the extension we proposed a viewing tower situated at the entrance of the stairs. The tower balanced the beautiful spire of St Martin's in the Fields and created a symmetrical composition of verticals flanking the National Gallery, reinforcing its horizontality and its focus on Nelson's column. Thus two independent, but crucial, public places were physically woven together, a new route was created and a new balanced composition established in the square, all by one relatively small building.

On a much larger scale, a competition project for a vast conference centre in the heart of Tokyo illustrates how looking beyond the confines of the brief to the broader context can generate new forms of public space and new forms of architecture. The brief specified three enormous conference halls, so we assessed the impact that such a mega-centre would have on the already congested site. Our conclusion was that, far from needing more building at ground level, the area – which was totally deprived of public space – would be better served by a series of open spaces offering room for public activities, for people simply to slow down and meet.

We proposed suspending the buildings six storeys up, thereby freeing the entire ground level and creating great covered outdoor spaces for public use. To achieve this, we worked closely with the brilliant engineer Peter Rice, of Ove Arup and Partners, on a structural solution that could suspend these great halls and meet the tremendously stringent anti-earthquake regulations governing all construction in Tokyo. Three giant silver capsules containing the conference halls, with room for 10,000 people, were suspended like ships in dry-dock over sheltered public spaces. Access to the halls and their roof gardens was by glazed travelator tubes that criss-crossed above the public spaces. The open plazas were stepped down from the street level and ringed with cafés, exhibition spaces, restaurants, cinemas and shops. The project evoked Japan's shipbuilding tradition and its remarkable industrial ability.

These two very public projects show how buildings can interact with the public domain. When buildings contribute to the public realm, they encourage people to meet and converse. They engage the passer-by. They stimulate rather than repress people's natural human potential. They humanise the city.

As well as framing public life, buildings serve the specific needs of the people who use them. This raises the practical question of how to design buildings to keep pace with people's requirements. Modern life is changing much faster than the buildings that house it. A building that is a financial market today may need to become an office in five years and a university in ten. So buildings that are easy to modify will have a longer useful life and represent a more efficient use of resources. But designing flexibility of use into our buildings inevitably moves architecture away from fixed and perfect forms. Classical architecture, for example, derives its beauty from its harmonious composition: nothing can be added to it, nothing taken away. But when society demands buildings capable of responding to

Centre Georges Pompidou
Piano + Rogers

▶ Building as public information screen. The Centre's indeterminate form allows for flexibilty of use.

Tokyo Forum competition
Richard Rogers Partnership

▶ A proposed new twenty-four hour meeting place for the people of Tokyo. A major extension of the public realm created by suspending the three giant halls in order to give the entire street level over to public use. Drawing showing the halls suspended like ships in dry dock. The multi-level streetscape provides access to restaurants, cafés, galleries and exhibitions.

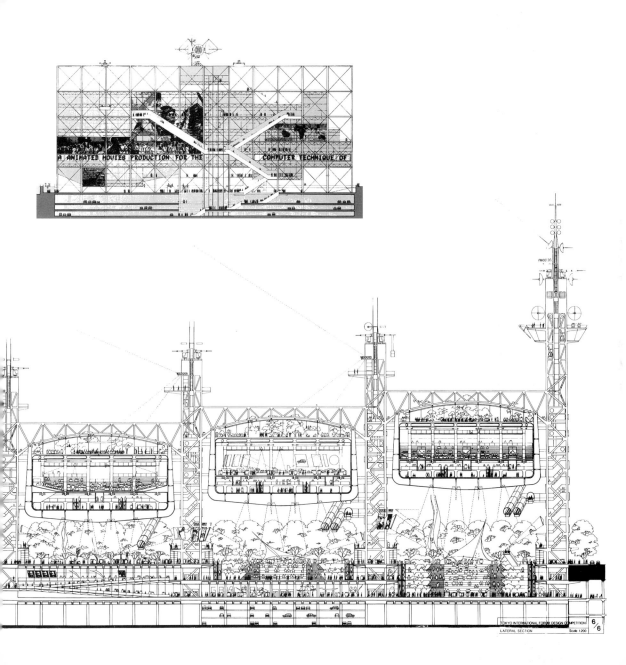

A ANIMATED MOVIES PRODUCTION FOR THE   COMPUTER TECHNIQUE OF

TOKYO INTERNATIONAL FORUM DESIGN COMPETITION
LATERAL SECTION   Scale 1:200

6/6

changing requirements, then we must provide flexibility and search for new forms that express beauty within adaptability.

My partner Renzo Piano and I designed the Pompidou Centre in Paris with this in mind. The building was conceived of not as a monument but as a people's place where different ages, interests and cultures can come together. The Centre houses facilities ranging from conference halls, cinemas and restaurants to libraries, concert halls and art galleries. We aimed to create a building that would not constrain the future arrangement of these facilities, but where the activities themselves would dictate the building's form over time. Our solution was a framework of spaces that could be added together or subtracted, opened up or divided. Placing all the structural columns, service ducts, lifts and corridors externally meant that the floors – each at its largest extent the size of two football pitches – were free of all obstacles. Access to activities was by a system of external public streets hung off the facade of the building. These were free for anyone to use and enjoy views of the piazza and the Parisian skyline. The escalators, 'streets in the air' and viewing platforms extended the public piazza up the façade of the building, and created a series of open terraces and glazed galleries where people could see and be seen.

The scale of a building is defined not by its size alone, but by the articulation of its parts. To reduce the apparent bulk of this large building, we created a façade that would catch and sculpt the light. It is a layered façade, not a wall but a series of transparent screens and metal structures, with terraces and balconies, one behind the other. In order to create a building that could be altered dramatically in unpredictable ways and still retain its coherence, we designed a kit of parts that could be assembled in different patterns: a stacked and ever-changing medieval village rather than a neo-classical temple.

Pompidou Centre
Piano + Rogers

People draw people

▲ Public spaces extend from the piazza accross the façade creating a multi-tiered public domain.
Richard Einzig – Arcaid

▶The public walkways and escalators draw visitors to the front doors of galleries and give dramatic views of Paris and the piazza.
Richard Einzig – Arcaid

Every generation needs to reinvent its public institutions and create new ones. The Pompidou Centre was as much an exploration of the concept of an adaptable, pluralist institution as it was an architectural exploration of flexible space and fragmented architectural form. New ideas require new forms, and this applies to buildings which house our daily needs as well as our institutions, be they homes, offices, universities, schools, hospitals or museums. Inflexible buildings hinder the evolution of society by inhibiting new ideas.

If new buildings must respond to the changing needs of society, then we must also consider how to adapt the vastly greater number of existing buildings. Leaving aside the conservation of the very greatest of buildings, the preservation of our general architectural heritage raises fundamental questions. Slavishly restoring old buildings to their supposed original condition is, I suggest, a misconception that goes against the very grain of traditional architecture. Buildings have always been adapted, reshaped, redecorated, replumbed and relit throughout their lives. But this organic process grinds to a halt in the face of over-zealous preservation. As a result, buildings become less flexible: they are more expensive to convert and can constrict new activity. Worse still is the practice of preserving the façade and constructing an entirely unrelated building behind it. This expedient solution to preservation reduces an interesting building to a historical shell – 'heritage' camouflaging a modern, and usually banal, commercial building.

By contrast, history shows us that even our very best buildings can be robustly modernised to respond to new needs. This can be done by creating a dialogue between old and new; here I am thinking of examples such as Scarpa's Castelvecchio in Verona or Norman Foster's Sackler Gallery at the Royal Academy in London. When contemplating the history of a building such as the Louvre – which has experienced almost continuous change for hundreds of years yet still retains its unity and speaks eloquently of every passing age – I marvel at the continuum of culture that has produced its present form, glass pyramid included. The work of I. M. Pei at the Louvre has proved that the finer the building, the greater the need for high quality response – quality of both thought and of execution.

Preserving the historical appearance of entire districts of cities is fraught with problems. Good contemporary work executed with skill and integrity can, in all but the most sensitive areas, complement its older neighbours more successfully than a modern building masquerading in historical costume. Juxtaposing new and old buildings is a practice that has a long and honourable history in our cities and towns.

In Britain, many of our cities revel in the contrast between medieval, Georgian and Gothic. There are sublime compositions, such as at King's College, Cambridge, where the great Gothic chapel that once stood alone in a meadow is now contrasted with classical buildings: buildings of one age proudly rising beside those of another. Superb examples outside Britain include the Piazza della Signoria in Florence, where Vasari's classical Uffizi Gallery communicates so powerfully with the medieval splendour of the Palazzo Vecchio. Or in Venice, where the effervescent Byzantine cathedral is framed by the elegant classical arcades of the Piazza San Marco. All testify to the value of a courageous approach that embraces change.

Traditional aesthetics based on buildings conforming with their neighbours need to be challenged. In the disconnected forms of a street in Tokyo, where to a westerner the only apparent unifying visual factors are the vertical signage banners and electronic information hoardings, which themselves are interrupted by the occasional religious temple, a beauty emerges out of the apparent chaos. Is it a *sine qua non* that we need protecting from the shock of the new?

Accumulation of culture

Old and new together creating
a harmonious composition of
complementary architectures
and adding new life to the
cultural heritage.

▲ The pyramid at the Louvre,
I.M. Pei architect.
Serge Hambourg

▶ King's College, Cambridge

▶ Piazza del Signoria,
Florence

Today, we are letting our architectural heritage choke our future. The departure of the British Library from the famous Reading Room at the British Museum, for example, offers an opportunity for refocusing the entire institution on this beautiful domed room and opening it up as a central public piazza. But scruples about changing the use of an important heritage building threaten this obvious but radical solution. We should not let the ghosts of the Reading Room block the natural contact between people, and constrain the reorganisation of our most prestigious cultural institution.

Preservation is obviously preferable to the demolition of a good building and its replacement by a poor one, but a building should not be preserved at the price of stifling innovation. The importance of breathing life into our architectural heritage cannot be overstated. Making museums of our cities ossifies society. The historian Roy Porter sums it up: *'When buildings take precedence over people, we get heritage, not history.'*

Breaking with preconceptions about architecture frees the architect to exploit new technologies and manufacturing techniques. Given the world-wide housing crisis, this issue can no longer be ignored. Embracing the use of new, recycled or composite materials can generate both cost savings and qualitative improvements. These innovative approaches to creating buildings can involve both high and low technology.

In 1991 we were approached by a Korean manufacturer who was targeting the enormous Korean and Asian residential market. Economic prosperity in Korea has prompted fundamental social change: young couples are moving out of the parental home, causing a steep demand for new residential accommodation. Demand for labour in the expanding manufacturing industries has left a critical shortfall of labour in the construction industry, further increasing the

▲ Tokyo street scene.
Mike Davis – Magnum

The shock of the new

▶ Daniel Libeskind's proposed extension to the Victoria and Albert Museum disregards good manners but adds drama and challenges the viewer to explore and compare.
Harry Gruyaert

cost of even poor quality housing. Our client was eager to explore the application of factory-based prefabrication techniques in the production of residential accommodation. A target was set that reduced the cost of delivery of a prefabricated single unit by some 80 per cent.

To achieve such an important reduction in cost implied considering the manufacture, construction and fit-out of every element of the residential unit from the structure to the glazing to the internal fittings. Working with the engineer Peter Rice, we developed a lightweight structural panel system using composites of recycled plastics and sheet metals. The basic element of the system was a single residential unit 'box', the size of a standard container, which could be assembled as low-rise, courtyard or high-rise configurations. Buyers would design the layout of their apartment, select the fittings and review the design on a computer-generated model. The customised unit was then fabricated and fully fitted-out in the factory. The completed unit was transported by truck and erected by computer-controlled cranes.

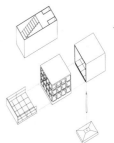

Contrasting with these high-technology processes, emergency housing was developed in Kobe, Japan, by the architect/engineer Shigeru Ban, using humble everyday materials and production techniques. The load-bearing systems of the walls, roofs and floors consisted of cardboard tubes made from layers of recycled paper. A house for four people can be erected in six hours. Since the successful application of this material in Kobe to provide housing and a local church, UNHCR has funded further exploration of its use for refugee camps. In these situations basic machinery is flown in that can produce paper tubes *in situ* out of existing waste materials.

I have been discussing how the public realm should shape buildings and how flexible buildings offer us new ways of organising our lives.

**Industrialised housing
system for Hanssem,
Korea, 1991**
Richard Rogers Partnership

Assembly-line, low cost, high-
quality housing aimed at the
rapidly expanding Asian
market.

▲ Site works are reduced to
assembly of prefabricated
units.

◄ Model of units arranged as
tower block.
Eamonn O'Mahony

◄ *page left*
Having selected the
components of the apartment,
a computer model creates an
instant on-screen visualisation
for the buyer.

Each apartment is fabricated
from a manufactured kit of
interchangeable components
assembled in the factory.

Typical arrangement of units
around a central lift core.

Emergency housing project using standard cardboard tubes, Kobe, Japan
Shigeru Ban, architect

▲ Cardboard tube chapel
Hiroyuki Hirai

▶ Lightweight structural components are easily assembled by unskilled workers. A single family dwelling takes just six hours to construct and can withstand hurricane-force winds.
Hiroyuki Hirai

▶ Exploded view of the dwelling: beer crate foundations, timber plank floors, cardboard tube walls and structure, canvas roof.
Hiroyuki Hirai

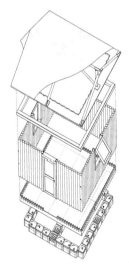

Both these concepts encourage a vibrant society and reinforce the social dimension of environmental sustainability. Now I want to describe how the implementation of sustainability will revolutionise the form of buildings and how this approach could be exploited by architects to humanise and beautify their buildings.

As we have seen, half of the energy derived from fossil fuels is consumed by buildings. According to *Scientific American*, the buildings of the industrialised countries consumed in 1985 an estimated $250 billion worth of energy. The challenge for architects is to develop buildings that incorporate sustainable technologies, and so reduce their pollution and running costs. Three-quarters of everyday energy use in buildings is accounted for, in more or less equal proportions, by artificial lighting, heating and cooling; but all these functions are now being revolutionised by new technology and new practices. Innovation is underway which can radically reduce long-term running costs and pollution generated by buildings.

Working with nature

▶ Autonomous house
research project
Aspen, Colorado, 1978.
Rogers Patscentre

The typical commercial office block, conceived during an era when the liberal use of cheap energy was the accepted way of meeting modern standards for working conditions, was designed to create a sealed internal environment that operated despite, rather than in conjunction with, the natural environment. This high-energy approach led to the creation of buildings with deep cross-sections and highly artificial internal environments. These large, densely occupied floors, together with the intensive use of computers and other machines, generate vast amounts of heat, requiring powerful equipment to extract the hot, stale air and pump in fresh, chilled, filtered and humidified air. In addition, the windows are so far from most people's desks that they need artificial lighting throughout the day. The result is an energy-guzzling environment that isolates people from nature, disconnects them from the life of the city and grossly pollutes the environment.

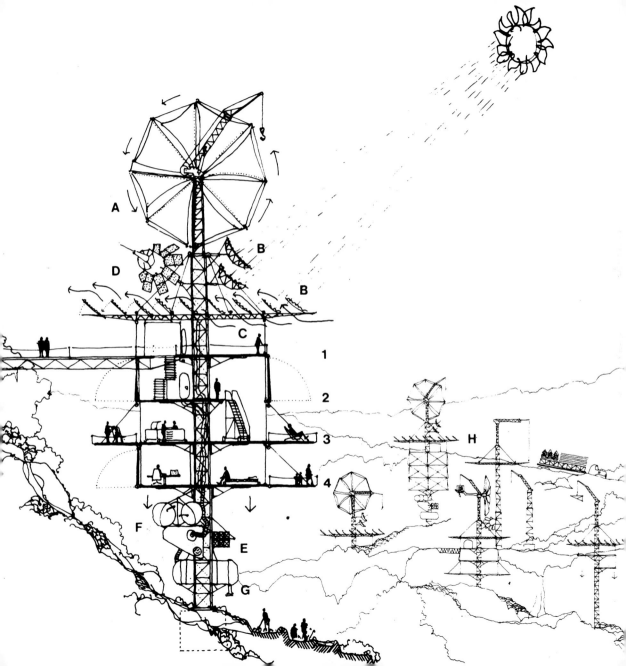

Inland Revenue competition proposal, 1992
Richard Rogers Partnership

◄ The roof profile is streamlined to encourage prevailing winds to draw air out of the building, thus reducing the need for mechanical ventilation. Landscaped enclosures filter and humidify fresh air before it enters the building.
Eamonn O'Mahony

◄ Section showing air movement during summer.

Changing our technologies and our expectations can dramatically reduce the energy consumption of a building – and halving the energy used by buildings would reduce overall global energy consumption by a quarter. At home and in old buildings, for example, we readily tolerate seasonal temperature variations. If today's office users, instead of insisting on a year-round temperature of 20°C, were also to accept mild seasonal variations, the building could be opened up to the outside environment and its reliance on air-conditioning significantly reduced. These practices can reduce energy consumption yet still provide a controlled environment. Architects are now relying less on 'active' high-energy technological solutions and are beginning to explore 'passive' technologies which use renewable energy harnessed from natural resources such as plants, wind, sun, earth and water.

In a competition brief for an Inland Revenue building in Nottingham a low-energy building was specified. We responded by investigating all the means available in nature for producing a temperate environment without resorting to mechanical systems and high-energy consumption. Two sides of the site were polluted and noisy. However, the other sides bordered a quiet canal, so we pushed the building to the edge of the roads and opened up a small public garden beside the canal. We placed the basic administration against the road, with social functions and communal facilities nestling around the new garden at the canal front.

The administration building was protected from the pollution and noise of the road by a metre-wide double-glazed wall, into which windows could be opened for ventilation. Between the two buildings we created a landscaped courtyard rather like a small ravine. The two rows of buildings were linked across this gently curving landscape by glazed bridges. This courtyard was not only the visual focus of the buildings, but also produced a micro-climate that conditioned the external air

used to ventilate the buildings. An average tree, for example, absorbs carbon dioxide, gives off oxygen, transpires 380 litres of water a day and purifies the air in its vicinity. In summer, trees give shade, limit heat-gain from the sun and reduce glare into buildings. Trees together with water, shrubs and plants compose a landscape that filters pollution, humidifies and cools the air.

Slimmer buildings allow more people to have windows close at hand, and reduce the need for artificial lighting. Inside the building, air that enters through openable windows can be circulated without using mechanical fans by shaping the ceilings and roofs aerodynamically and by connecting floors to a larger space or atrium: as the air in the atrium rises in temperature, the 'stack effect' pulls air upwards, sucking the stale air out of the peopled spaces. Buildings that are divided by an atrium can contain large floors, with good visual contact between people and healthy ventilation.

The roof profile can be shaped to respond and in some cases trap prevailing winds. In certain climates and conditions this can increase the natural draw of air out of the building and produce comfortable environmental conditions without the need for high-energy mechanical cooling systems.

Law courts that we are designing in the city centre of Bordeaux apply similar principles of natural ventilation in a hot European climate. The need for good circulation of fresh air in the courtrooms influenced the design of their shape. They function and look rather like oast-houses: letting air in from below and light but little heat through a small efficient skylight. Heat from the sun at the top of the courts increases the stack effect and generates enough air movement to dispense with mechanical fans. Before the air enters the courtrooms it crosses an external pool and is cooled and humidified. The public hall in which the seven courtrooms stand is

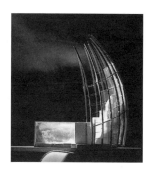

New Caledonian Cultural Centre
Renzo Piano Building Workshop

▲Wind tunnel testing of air movement under prevailing wind conditions.

◀ Renzo Piano is building a cultural centre in New Caledonia. The forms are designed to respond to the local climatic conditions of heat and intense humidity. The result is a series of roof and building profiles that are designed to shade, cool and ensure a constant flow of ventilation in the public areas.
M. Denance

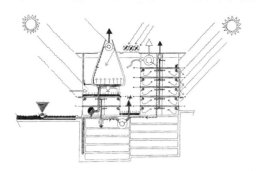

**Law Courts, Bordeaux,
France, 1992–98**
Richard Rogers Partnership

▲ Section showing the
natural flow of air through the
building.

▲ The public façade of the
court building is the glazed
Hall with its seven free-
standing courtrooms.
Eamonn O'Mahony

▶ The courtrooms are shaped
by the need to encourage
natural ventilation and provide
good daylighting without
generating unacceptable levels
of solar gain.
Eamonn O'Mahony

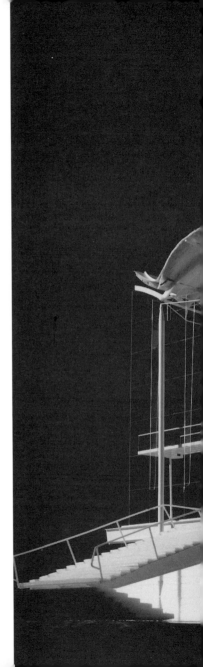

shaded but fully glazed. It overlooks the pool and beyond it the great medieval cathedral. The hall draws its air across the pool, but also cool energy from constant-temperature groundwater which is circulated through heat-exchangers. This natural air-conditioning system is part of an architectural composition that provides views and reflections for those inside and that can also be seen and enjoyed by those on the outside.

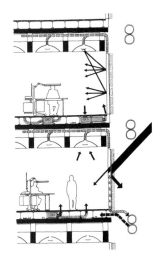

The 'cool energy' of night air can be stored in the internal structure of a building. The Lloyd's of London Market building, for example, has both a glazed triple skin for insulation and an exposed internal concrete ceiling that absorbs cool energy overnight and sheds it during the day. This exploitation of the thermal mass of a building reduces the need for artificial cooling during day-time occupation. These techniques are merely reinterpretations of devices that have been used for thousands of years. The way a building faces in relation to the sun is vital to the design of a low-energy building. Low-energy techniques commonly reduce the total commercial energy consumption of a building by between a half and three-quarters. Fortunately, Britain's temperate environment is well suited to these techniques.

The concept of a glazed double skin can be expanded to enclose an entire building in a layer of air, providing an all-enveloping glass 'chimney'. Two glass skins reduce the impact of pollution and noise on a building, and allow windows built into the inner skin to be opened onto the transparent vent. From there, stale air is drawn out by stack effect and by prevailing winds flowing over the outer surfaces of the building. In summer the vent can be opened to increase the airflow and shed as much heat as possible. In winter the system is closed down to increase insulation and trap heat.

Lloyd's of London
Richard Rogers Partnership

▲ Plan of Lloyd's showing separation of short- and long-life elements for easy adaptability

◀ The Atrium is the heart of the Market, but also the exhaust system for stale air from the trading floors.
The exposed concrete structure of columns, beams and ceilings is an integral part of the cooling system, storing night-time cool and absorbing day-time heat.
Alastair Cook

◀ *page left*
Triple-glazing provides a highly insulated skin to the building. Heat from within the window depth, generated by the sun, is drawn out and stored in basement tanks, reducing the need for cooling office spaces. Translucent glass screens reduce solar gain and create a wall of light. Openable clear glass panels give the individual occupants control over their environment.

The highly articulated façade is generated by the components of the structure and servicing.
Richard Bryant, Arcaid

A solar-powered car is built to transport a driver as efficiently as possible using only renewable energy. To do this, it must minimise its confrontation with natural forces. Architecture too needs to minimise its confrontation with nature. To do that it must respect nature's laws. Buildings can be contoured to reduce drag and air turbulence. Architecture is becoming more streamlined and responsive as its forms interact with natural forces.

In a recent research project for offices in Tokyo, we were asked to explore the idea of energy self-sufficiency. We began by cutting to a minimum the energy required by the building. All spaces were naturally lit. Deep spaces and basements that needed additional lighting used daylight that was concentrated and piped through fibre-optic cables. Groundwater was circulated to cool the structure of the building. The south façade was clad in electronic glass, which is translucent when the sun is shining – keeping out direct light – and transparent when it is overcast.

The dynamic computer programs we used to model the flow of air through and around the building had been developed for the aeronautical and automotive industries. They enabled us to test ways of using prevailing winds to improve the draw of air out of the building's tower. Pushing the issue further, we next explored the possibility of adjusting the shape of the building so that the wind moved faster over its surfaces. This eventually led us to apply the principle that creates 'lift' on an aeroplane's wing. The shape of the building accelerated prevailing winds through turbines located between the building and its adjoining tower. These turbines converted the wind energy into electricity – electricity used to power the building's services during the day, and the national grid at night. Our engineers measured the building's energy use over the course of a year and showed that it achieved overall energy self-sufficiency: it produced as much energy as it consumed. Here again, computer

Turbine Tower Project
Tokyo, Japan 1993
Richard Rogers Partnership

▲ Concept sketch. Wind turbines mounted between the building and its lift tower, convert wind energy into electricity.

▶ Laboratory wind tunnel tests of the Turbine Tower show that power is generated by the turbines under varied prevailing wind conditions.

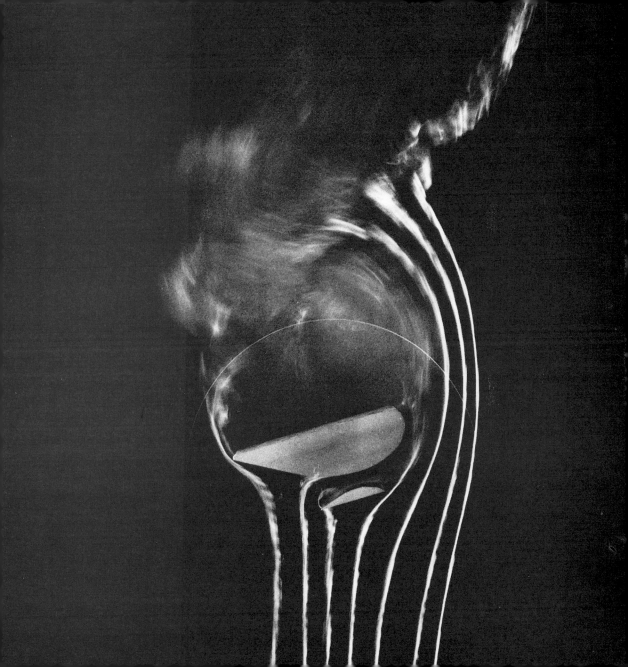

technology is the breakthrough which has revolutionised the process of designing low-energy buildings. Programs already available can generate models that predict the air movement, light levels and heat gain in a building while it is still on the drawing board. This significantly increases our ability to refine those aspects of the building's design that can use the natural environment to reduce its energy consumption. New technology is also giving buildings increasingly sensitive electronic 'nervous systems', able to register internal and external conditions and respond to specific needs. New materials exist that can change from high insulation to low, from opaque to transparent, that can react organically to the environment and transform themselves in response to daily and seasonal cycles.

The future is here, but its impact on architecture is only just beginning. Working our buildings into the cycle of nature will return architecture to its very roots.

Responsive skins

▲ Chameleon
Nick MacCrae

◄ Insulation, transparency and shading vary according to season, time and user needs. Experimental research.
Mike Davies architect

4   London: the humanist city

Without power and independence towns can contain good subjects, but they cannot have active citizens.

Alexis de Tocqueville

4

For four centuries London has been one of the world's most powerful financial, commercial and cultural centres. The legacy of this power and prosperity can be seen throughout the city: in its architecture, parks, squares, museums and public institutions. Even today London is rivalled only by New York in terms of extent and diversity of economic and cultural activity. But London since the early 1980s has failed to convince even its own citizens that it can offer a healthy, secure and humanising environment: a sobering contrast to the London of the early 1930s that gave my Italian parents and many others political refuge, and was universally respected for its civility.

London was the first city to create a civic administration capable of co-ordinating the complex matrix of modern urban services, ranging from public transport to housing, from water to education, from parks to museums. If Westminster was the Mother of Parliaments, then the London County Council (LCC) was acknowledged in my parents' time to be the most progressive metropolitan authority in the world. London's red double-decker buses, its police force and its pioneering underground network, its schools and council housing, showed a city committed to creating a humanist environment.

This was a great achievement, considering that only fifty years earlier London had been the worst slum city of the industrialised world: overcrowded, polluted and ridden with disease, a city in which life expectancy was barely twenty-five years. In 1883 the clergyman Andrew Mearns gave a vivid account of the urban slums of Victorian London: 'You grope your way along dark and filthy passages swarming with vermin. Then, if you are not driven back by the intolerable stench, you may gain admittance to the dens in which these thousands of beings herd together often two families in each room.'

Public outcry, campaigns in the press and irrepressible Victorian self-confidence propelled the transformation of the city, achieved through inspired planning legislation and the creation in 1889 of the LCC.

This pioneering approach to the management of London's environment survived until 1985, when the Conservative government, rather than attempting to reform the Greater London Council (GLC), successor to the LCC, abolished it in an act of politically motivated spite. The GLC's abolition meant that its responsibilities, most crucially the overall strategic planning for London, was then divided between five government departments, thirty-two London boroughs, the City of London, and some sixty committees and quangos.

The first modern European capital with an elected authority is now the only capital without one. Londoners have no elected representation, no direct say in their city's affairs, no foil to counter the development of the city for profit alone. London continues to be transformed by urban policies designed to empower the market rather than its citizens. With no overall co-ordination, London is failing to safeguard the quality of life of its citizens and its public transport system, and has shown itself incapable of even competing with other British cities to host international events. London lost its sense of unity, direction and pride. Rudderless and polluted, this great city's future hangs in the balance.

Elsewhere, city authorities have sought to manage change for the benefit of the citizen by vigorously investing in the future, by strengthening the public domain and embarking on ambitious programmes of urban regeneration. This has meant investment in state-of-the-art public transport and new cultural institutions, and promoting the development of mixed-use neighbourhoods. Throughout Europe, in fact, there is an emphasis on renewing urban culture and improving the quality of urban life.

London's lacklustre attitude towards planning its future provides a stark contrast. London continues to develop without participation or guiding vision, a situation worsened by the fact that its civic administration is in disarray. Taking control of the city's destiny will require widespread involvement in the debate about London's future. An elected authority accountable to Londoners is essential: only such a body can provide an administrative framework capable of implementing positive change, and enable all citizens to contribute to the development of an overall strategic plan for their city's future.

A new London authority needs to learn from past experience. Much of the day-to-day administration should remain with the individual boroughs and under the scrutiny of local people, but decisions on such strategic issues as metropolitan transport, housing, the public realm, culture, education, waste and recycling, pollution and taxation should be made by the elected body representing the entire city. Ultimately, there should be a hierarchy of decision-making that progresses from the citizen to the neighbourhood, to the borough, to the city, to the region and finally to the international scale.

I propose to use London as a case study to demonstrate that the transformation of British cities is possible. London is at a turning point in its history, and our generation has the opportunity of transforming it into one of the most habitable and civilised cities in the world.

As a society, we are shamefully ignorant of the positive impact that architecture and the design of cities can have on our lives. We need to make far-reaching changes in our approach to the built environment, and should be prepared to legislate for them. Education is one important component in remedying this situation, and a new system of participatory planning is essential. We need to establish new institutions where different interests involved in planning can meet. Just as the Victorians built public libraries to tackle illiteracy, so we should build Architecture Centres to involve and inform citizens, architects, planners and developers in designing the city to meet the needs of future generations.

Architecture Centres should be the venue for public debates on strategic plans, architectural competitions and planning applications. These local centres should exhibit adaptable working models of the borough and its neighbourhood; they should hold lectures, exhibitions and courses about the city, its architecture and its ecology. Planning committees should include citizens and specialists in all fields of urban design, because we need to focus the energy of all those with a stake in the urban environment on jointly tackling the problems of the city. At these centres the citizen could meet the developers and the planning committee its electorate. In effect they would need to be 'electronic town halls', both multi-media forums and physical meeting places, providing interaction and access to a broad range of information – a vehicle for the citizen to learn and to ensure that the planning professions serve the needs of the public.

'Realising the untapped wealth of knowledge and ideas which lie within the citizenry is the key to solving urban problems. A tapping of this wealth not only propels the city designers into unthought-of regions of ideas but serves the crucial purpose of assuring the citizens that their ideas and knowledge are an integral part of the solution. This approach is more than participation and consultation; it is co-operation, and co-operation reduces tension.' The architect Brian Anson writes here from experience, having championed citizens' rights against the property developers in Covent Garden in the 1960s.

From the early 1980s central government effectively excluded this type of participatory, planned approach in favour of a market-led approach that waits for developers to select sites and apply for planning permission. The market drive is profit. This approach tends to favour out-of-town sites or fields on the edge of the green belt, where land is cheap and where investment can be written off quickly;

during the boom of the 1980s it was quite common for companies to seek to recoup their investment in as little as four years. Inevitably many commercial planning applications are for single-function complexes such as retail, housing, offices or light industry: developments that merely meet an immediate commercial demand. The community's longer-term need for public space and mixed function is ignored, and with it the chance to create living neighbourhoods, sustainable communities.

The result of the market-led approach was most clearly illustrated by the redevelopment of the defunct docklands on the Isle of Dogs, where an extraordinary act of central government intervention removed control of the area's development from the local authorities. In its place the London Docklands Development Corporation (LDDC) was established, statutory planning regulations were suspended and tax incentives put in place to encourage development. Crucially, the nature of the development was encouraged to respond solely to market demand.

The result is an over-abundance of office space, a haphazard mix of commercial development, clumps of offices intermixed with clusters of housing. It is unsustainable development without real civic quality or lasting communal benefit. The money central government spent indirectly to encourage this development made it an extremely expensive fiasco for the taxpayer, who subsidised big business but had no say in how the money was spent. Government gave massive development tax relief to big business and also had to pay the lion's share of infrastructure costs. Instead of gaining a vibrant and humane new borough that would have taken its place within the larger framework of the metropolis and enriched the poorer communities in its vicinity, Londoners acquired a chaos of commercial buildings and the City footed the bill for one of the most spectacular bankruptcies of the 1990s. Ironically for the government, bankers and Londoners,

had there been a balance of offices, homes, schools, shops and social amenities, the Isle of Dogs would have been less affected by the crash in the office market.

Even in areas where planning regulations have applied, the planning process has been, as far as the citizen is concerned, reactive rather than pro-active. Imprecise planning guidelines, unpredictable and often ill-informed planning committees, and the lack of productive public consultation during the design process often leads to expensive public inquiries and the taking of piecemeal decisions by the Secretary of State. The planning system was set up over fifty years ago. It is a slow, expensive process, and its attempts at aesthetic control have failed to achieve any advantages over cities that have a less prescriptive approach.

In tandem with planning for buildings and open spaces, an overall strategic plan co-ordinates environmental policies – policies to help streamline the 'metabolism' of London by reducing its consumption of energy and resources, recycling its waste, reusing its spent energy, reducing its pollution of air, land and water. In environmental terms London is one of the least sustainable cities in Europe. A recent report carried out by Herbert Girardet, Professor of Environmental Planning at Middlesex University, lists London's massive consumption of resources, among them: in one year the equivalent of 110 supertanker loads of oil, 1.2 million tons of timber, 1.2 million tons of metal, 2 million tons each of food, plastics and paper, and 1 billion tons of water; in return the city's production of waste in a year includes 15 million tons of rubbish, 7.5 million tons of sewage and 60 million tons of carbon dioxide. In all, though London covers just 400,000 acres it requires nearly 50 million acres to provide it with resources and absorb its waste. Herbert Giradet puts it very clearly: 'Although [London] contains only 12 per cent of Britain's population, it requires an area equivalent to all the

Boom-and-bust commercial planning

▲ Canary Wharf, London. London gained a major concentration of commercial office space but could have gained a thriving mixed community.
Edward Sykes – Independent

◄ Laissez-faire planning: commercial buildings, roads and left-over spaces.
Peter Baistow

country's productive land to service it – though this extends to the wheat prairies of Kansas, the tea gardens of Assam, the copper mines of Zambia and other far-flung places.'

Like all major cities, London presents an environmental threat to the ecology of the earth. Reducing urban consumption, waste and pollution is central to combating the environmental crisis and provides the basis for the creation of a healthy and efficient quality of city life. The importance of implementing an overall strategic plan for London which incorporates architectural, environmental, transport and social criteria cannot be overestimated.

In the short term London must consolidate rather than expand further. As in industrialised cities all over the world, London's industries have departed, its docks have been abandoned, many of its neighbourhoods have collapsed, and yet pollution and congestion have increased. Over the last thirty years, central London has lost almost a third of its population and 20 per cent of its jobs, more than any other major capital in Europe. But while the city population has declined, the population of outer London has increased, sprawling outwards in an ever-widening circle. London, some thirty miles wide in 1945, is now served by a commuter belt 200 miles wide stretching from Cambridge to Southampton, and is the largest and most complex urban region in Europe.

Brian Anson has described London's predicament: 'London like so many cities has an internationally known core, an inner ring, and an outer ring tending to a green belt. Whilst the city's core suffers from problems of pollution and congestion it is the inner ring in which the poor and disadvantaged are trapped. They can't escape to the outer ring nor afford the facilities of the inner core. It is here that the poor have pushed out by gentrification and it is here that social services such as hospitals, schools and transport have been reduced. This is the powder keg of the city. Nearly all city planning of recent times has concentrated on the core. This is an enormous fallacy and possibly a recipe for disaster. The trickle-down theory simply does not work.'

As London has spread out and its industries have deserted the city, huge disparities of wealth have resulted. In Britain the gap between rich and poor is the widest in Europe: the richest 1 per cent own 18 per cent of the nation's wealth, a situation that provokes both despair and crime. Though London is one of the richest cities in the world it has seven of the ten most deprived boroughs in the country, most of them in east London. Five per cent of inner London is derelict: large stretches of Wandsworth, Vauxhall, Greenwich, Shepherd's Bush, Lambeth, Hoxton, Waterloo and King's Cross. These desolate, often contaminated wastelands are a social hazard as well as an environmental blight. They are ugly and alienating for those who live on their peripheries. Though the remediation costs dissuade market-led redevelopment, they offer magnificent opportunity for growth that would regenerate existing communities and underpin the future sustainability of the capital.

Historically, London, unlike the walled cities of its European counterparts, developed around a multitude of centres, and it is still a collection of distinct towns and villages – Hampstead to Westminster, Notting Hill to Limehouse – each with its own local character, visual identity and history. Instead of allowing London to sprawl, and this polycentric pattern to erode, we should actively reinforce these neighbourhoods as compact, sustainable nuclei.

John Gummer, the Secretary of State for the Environment between 1993 and 1997, introduced radical new policy guidelines. In particular Public Policy Guidance 13 establishes a strategic preference for increasing inner-city development densities and focusing development on existing, often polluted inner-city sites before allowing development of further green field sites. It also calls for the co-ordination of development with public transport to reduce dependence on private car use. These policies will potentially reverse the tide of sprawl and consolidate London's polycentric structure of compact neighbourhoods. They represent a sea change in British planning and need to be applied in the local authorities with conviction and flair.

Along the Thames, from Woolwich in the east to Brentford in the west, London has vast areas of derelict industrial land that could help meet the capital's huge predicted demand for housing. These abandoned docklands and industrial sites provide a new generation with the ideal opportunity to reinstate the river as the focus of London life. International architects and – planners of the highest calibre should be invited to prepare flexible masterplans – including environmental impact analysis – that cover major derelict areas due for redevelopment. If, for example, the large groups of empty sites bordering the Thames were subject to flexible masterplanning studies their eventual redevelopment would create important additions to the public realm, be it as esplanades, a series of distinct parks along the river or simply fine compositions of buildings and spaces. The coherence and beauty of the whole would be the object of the plan, without sacrificing the flexibility of any particular development.

Future architects and developers of individual sites would be guided by overall strategic criteria set down in the masterplan, and not by bland, generic guidelines or the constrictive prescriptions of an aesthetic formula. This is how long-term public requirements can lead private development, without impinging unduly on the autonomy of the eventual developer or architect. It is in the public's interest to create long-term quality in the city – which is why it is the public's responsibility to ensure coherent planning. Planning for the future of London requires government direction, the procurement of the best designers and the active involvement of the citizen.

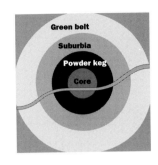

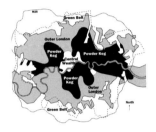

A social plan of London

▲ Diagram showing how poverty is concentrated in the inner ring between the historic core and suburbia developments.

▲ London has 14 of the 20 poorest boroughs in England.

▶ Diagram showing how targeting urban renewal projects should improve the quality of life in disadvantaged areas and facilitate their integration into the city.

Urban renewal projects target London's areas of poverty

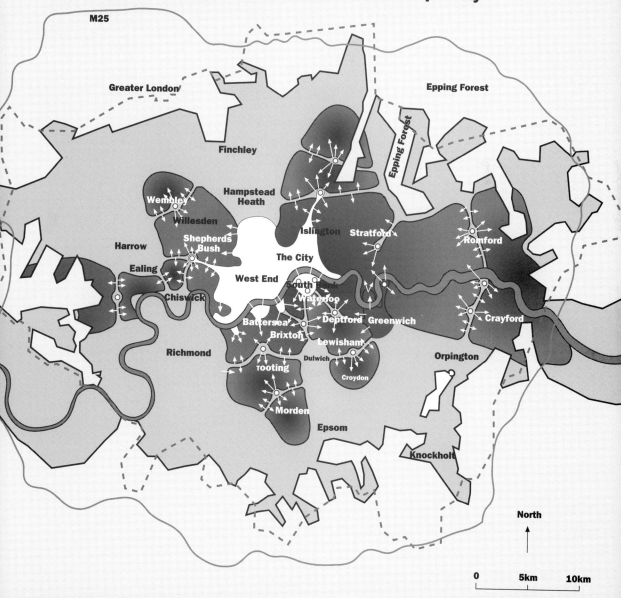

M25

Greater London

Epping Forest

Epping Forest

Finchley

Hampstead
Heath

Wembley

Willesden

Islington

Stratford

Romford

Harrow

Shepherds
Bush

The City

Ealing

West End

South Bank

Chiswick

Waterloo

Deptford

Greenwich

Crayford

Battersea

Brixton

Lewisham

Richmond

Tooting

Dulwich

Orpington

Croydon

Morden

Epsom

Knockholt

North

0   5km   10km

East London, which contains the greatest concentration of poverty and dereliction, must be a particular subject of the strategic plan. It is here that London will become inseparably linked to Europe through the international rail network, and the commercial significance of this link can hardly be exaggerated – think of the effect that Heathrow airport has had on London's expansion to the west. Growth to the east will inevitably take place, it is up to us to manage it for the long-term needs of London. And when London needs to expand further, then this should be in large self-contained urban clusters connected to new public high-speed transport links.

I am convinced that if the right lessons are drawn from recent experience, London could be radically transformed for the better. The anti-social pattern of piecemeal growth engendered by development motivated solely by profit has shown itself inadequate to London's needs. Strategic planning and specific masterplan studies provide the key to capitalising on the availability of so many redevelopment sites, and making a concerted renaissance of the city.

Peter Hall, Professor of Urban design at the London School of Economics, presents startling figures for housing demand in South-east England: 'Just under 7 million of us live in London now; another 11.5 million live in the South East beyond the M25: that is 18.5 million people in all in 7 million separate households. We now face an explosion of the need for new households: in the next twenty years, 1.64 million more in the South East: a 23 per cent increase.' High-quality affordable housing is desperately needed to respond to this.

As it is, on a typical night in 1995 more than 2000 people were sleeping rough on the streets of the capital. It is a shocking indictment that in the same year London's authorities built only 300 new homes. One hundred and twenty thousand people, including

A sustainable development framework applied to formerly industrial land

Greenwich Peninsula Master Plan, 1996
Richard Rogers Partnership

The site, complete with new Jubilee Line underground station and London Transport Interchange, is being decontaminated and a framework of urban infrastructure constructed that will act as platform for the National Millennium Exhibition in the short term and leave the foundation of a compact, mixed use neighbourhood.

The public infrastructure will include over 50 acres of public open space, parks, squares and riverwalk; roads, streets and public utilities. The first phases of development will see 3,000 housing units of which one quarter will be 'assisted'.
Richard Davies

families with children, are living in London without the security of a permanent home; that is more than the entire population of one of London's average boroughs. Government housing policy since the 1980s actually undermined the diversity of communities and encouraged city sprawl.

Housing is one of the keys to consolidating the neighbourhoods of our city. The way to meet the huge demand and to strengthen our existing communities is to redevelop derelict and brown land to produce dense, compact and mixed developments based around public transport nodes. If we want to reinforce our neighbourhoods and grow sustainably, then London needs to create communities that offer an affordable and humane quality of life.

New housing in London, even when it is partially funded by the taxpayer, is built by private developers or private associations. Their developments are designed to satisfy consumer demand rather than to consolidate neighbourhoods. As a result dense schemes with public streets, squares and parks, that mix shops, workplaces and schools – the model of a sustainable community – are rejected in favour of compounds that cram the maximum number of individual houses onto the site. This approach merely perpetuates London's environmentally unsustainable low-density sprawl. The British persist in regarding 'housing' as an autonomous issue. We ignore the proven advantage of integrating housing policy into an overall urban strategy.

In countries such as the Netherlands, housing is acknowledged to be a major factor of urban regeneration. It is designed with the participation of residents and expressly includes facilities that contribute to the vibrancy of the whole community. Public housing is built by self-governing housing associations, co-ordinated by the local authority and integrated with privately owned housing. Tenants and local people are involved in the entire process of procuring new housing, from the selection of the architect to the planning of the scheme.

In London there are large areas of unoccupied space above shops and in unused office buildings. Organisations such as LOTS (Living Over The Shop) claim that at least 200,000 permanent homes could be provided above shops and commercial premises in inner London alone. London's 20 million square feet of unused office space could theoretically provide a further 20,000 units.

London must also relieve the despair of the hundreds of thousands of poorer people trapped in its decaying housing estates. More than a quarter of all families in inner London live in local authority housing. The typical council estates of the 1960s and 1970s are 'anti-city' in their layout and notoriously badly run. They have isolated their occupants from the rest of the community and condemned them to neglect. By training residents to manage their own estates, agencies such as the National Tenants Resource Centre are turning despair into hope. Estates such as Broadwater Farm, Clapton Park or Hornsey, formerly places of unacceptable degradation, have been transformed by partnerships between housing authorities and residents backed by local knowledge and resources. This grassroots movement must be encouraged: it should be sponsored by central government and informed by good practice from abroad.

Bringing residents back to the city centre is an essential objective of sustainable planning, but housing strategies that encourage inner city living must be supported by policies which improve the quality of air, the safety of the streets, education and mobility in the city.

The private motor vehicle is a further contributing cause of London's ills. Pollution caused by cars contributes to the fact that one in seven London children suffers from asthma or another respiratory condition. During the winter of 1994 record levels of pollution were blamed for 155 deaths in just four days. Something like 10,000 people die each year in the UK because of emissions from vehicles; this pollution is said to add £3.9 billion per annum to the nation's medical bill. Stephen Joseph of Transport 2000 reckons that the car industry has now reached the point which the tobacco industry reached thirty years ago: 'The health dimension is now changing the nature of the debate.'

But the motor vehicle is not just a problem because of the pollution it causes. Fear of traffic has an insidious effect on our behaviour and along with air quality is a major factor motivating families to move away from the centre of cities. Parents are loath to let young children cross the road on their own – a constraint that effectively isolates children from their friends, makes them less independent and retards their maturity. In the past twenty-five years the number of seven- and eight-year-olds who go to school on their own has fallen from 80 per cent to 9 per cent. Traffic and pollution is also discouraging pedestrians and cyclists. Only 9 per cent of British children now cycle to school, compared 83 per cent in Holland. And, as if pollution and congestion were not bad enough in themselves, the Confederation of British Industry estimates that in 1995 alone traffic congestion cost London £15 billion in wasted energy and time.

Furthermore, current policies favour an increase rather than a decrease in the use of cars. The separation of shopping, working and living, and the deterioration of public transport, have made the car an indispensable means of transport. New superstores, business parks, residential compounds and shopping centres are being located away from the community; large retail outlets drain business and life from the high street, and their location in peripheral areas gives rise to ever more traffic.

Cycle lanes

◀ Cycling in London is fraught with danger from congestion and pollution. Nor is this helped by the fact that London's public bus system is diesel-fuelled and contributes significantly to the poor air quality on its roads.

In 1995 the Department of the Environment admitted that the government's policy of allowing out-of-town shopping centres has brought commercial ruin to our market towns – a consequence that was already proven forty years ago in the USA. But London's towns and villages have suffered just as much, their smaller high street businesses crippled by high rents and rates and the polluted and congested streets. Individual boroughs are fighting back, trying to improve the physical environment and commercial vitality of their streets. This approach must be supported by business incentives for those who stay on and help to reinforce the community – in other words, affirmative action. This does not mean regulating the retail industry, but introducing a taxation structure that encourages services which sustain the broader community.

The government failed to tackle the problem of cars, even though it conceded that they are the major source of air pollution and that their numbers are set to rise. Already a staggering two-thirds of all journeys within London are made by car, and government sources predict that vehicular traffic will increase by 142 per cent over the next twenty-five years. Perversely, as the number of journeys by car increases, so the total number of people using the roads in buses and cars actually decreases. A comparison of the numbers using the London highways in the morning rush hour reveals a staggering decrease in users from 404,000 in 1956 to 251,000 in 1996.

Yet in recent years major public transport initiatives have been shunned. The Department of Transport's spending priorities have illustrated this perfectly: 97 per cent of its budget has gone on road transport and only 2 per cent on railways. Compare a 1930s underground map with one of the 1990s and you will see that they are basically the same: with the belated exception of the Jubilee Line extension, new lines, such as the Chelsea line or Crossrail, continue to be delayed or simply abandoned. The London Transport chairman

The public realm

Part of a series of analytical drawings showing the state of London's public realm.

The quality of life in the neighbourhoods is directly related to the number and quality of public interventions: squares, parks, leisure, culture, shopping and public transport

▶ Overlapping ten-minute catchment zones to the nearest underground station. Areas in black indicate lack of overlapping service.

Richard Rogers Partnership

400m/ 5mins
Underground

1Km/ 10 mins walk
from commuter head

0.5km

0.5km

1km

Peter Ford has recently stated that the 1997 budget cuts will have the effect of increasing the £1.2 billion backlog by £300 million a year for the next three years. Necessary upgrading of the Northern, District and Piccadilly lines will be delayed, and modernisation projects for stations at Elephant & Castle, Oxford Circus or Notting Hill Gate are simply being shelved.

Across the Channel, cities as diverse as Naples, Strasbourg and Athens are addressing congestion and pollution with far more courage and vision than London. Here, although we may have defined the problem accurately, the government has been unaccountably reluctant to implement solutions that are well within our technological and organisational competence. For example, Londoners who buy small-engine cars with catalytic converters – or, better still, electric cars – should be given tax benefits. Road pricing should be introduced to deter cross-town traffic; research suggests that this might bring about a 30 per cent reduction in traffic, but only if there were parallel improvements to public transport.

Increasingly, London boroughs are making life harder for the motorist by calming traffic, enforcing parking restrictions and increasing parking charges. Privatising the task of enforcement has created a huge increase in revenue from fines. The City of Westminster is using these resources to finance improvements to the public realm. But policies that simply restrict the use of private cars without taking corresponding action to improve public transport merely increase the cost of mobility and reduce the efficiency of Londoners. The government must make mobility affordable: average ticket prices on London's public transport are now 25 per cent more than those in Paris and twice those in Madrid.

4
124

Free public transport for all Londoners – why not? Services could be partially financed by a metropolitan tax levied on residents and employers (with the normal subsidies for senior citizens and people who are unemployed or on low incomes continuing). Residents and workers who paid the tax would receive a yearly travel card, while visitors would still need to buy tickets in the usual way. As public transport would be effectively free at the point of use to all taxpayers, travelling by car would begin to be perceived as a luxury. This would encourage people off the roads. Even the 24 per cent decrease in fare prices in the 1983 GLC 'Fare's Fair' initiative increased public transport's passenger miles by 16 per cent and reduced commuting by car. Reducing car traffic makes buses faster and more efficient and encourages cyclists. The short-term increase in demand could be eased by the purchase of more buses while long-term public transport projects such as trams, light rail and underground lines are built.

The design of neighbourly cities starts with integrated transport systems. London needs a strategy that co-ordinates all transportation systems: from the private to the public, from the riverbus to the tram and from new tube lines to bicycle paths. The viability of the whole system and each component should be evaluated in ecological and social terms, not just in terms of its profitability. Travel by car is currently cheap because it is subsidised by the taxpayer. The indirect costs of motoring – the building and maintenance of roads, the subsidies for company cars, the long-term damage caused by pollution, the disruption to the local community, the ill health – are simply not reflected in the cost of cars or petrol.

We are used to being told that large-scale expenditure on public transport is unjustifiable. But there are economists of all political persuasions who reject this notion. An effective public transport infrastructure will be useful to society for decades, possibly centuries to come. Its cost must be measured against the long-term benefit to the city, its workforce and its families. Good public transport will make London more competitive and energy efficient, and Londoners more mobile and healthier. And it can make our city more neighbourly and more beautiful.

Cities are first and foremost the meeting-place of people. Yet a large proportion of London's public domain, including almost all its streets and squares, are now dominated by the motor vehicle: these are places designed to respond to the needs of traffic and marred visually by its signage. Grand spaces like Parliament Square, Piccadilly Circus, Trafalgar Square, Hyde Park Corner and Marble Arch have all been overwhelmed by cars. The situation is even worse in local centres such as Hammersmith, Shepherd's Bush, Brixton, Dalston or the Elephant & Castle.

But the Londoner is waking up to the fact that citizens throughout Europe from Stockholm and Copenhagen to Athens and Rome are successfully reclaiming public spaces for their own communal use. Inspired mayors have pedestrianised their city centres and redesigned them as places for people. We too must take radical steps to redesign the public domain of the city.

A shift in government investment from private to public transport will give Londoners the opportunity to swap highways for public places. The experience of the 'ring of plastic' around the City of London is particularly encouraging. As an emergency measure to counter terrorism, the Corporation of London placed severe restrictions on through traffic – and proved that the commercial viability of a city centre does not rely on its accessibility by car. Moreover, the scheme has improved air quality and has reduced both road casualties and crime. In fact it is so popular with city workers that it is now being extended and made permanent. This is the first major sign of inspired leadership actively wresting control of the public domain from the central control of the Department of Transport.

Streets for people

▲ 'Reclaim the Streets' anti-car demonstrations focus attention on re-balancing the use of streets in favour of the pedestrian.
Adrian Fisk

▶ 'Critical Mass'. On the last Friday of each month over 1,000 cyclists take to the streets in central London during the peak rush hour bringing traffic to a standstill. In this way they hope to encourage travellers to use public transport or to cycle to work.
Adrian Fisk

Imagine the results if a similar restriction of traffic were applied to other important London spaces.

In 1986 we exhibited proposals for Trafalgar Square, the Embankment and the linking of the north and south banks of the Thames at Hungerford Bridge in our 'London as It Could Be' exhibition. These proposals demonstrated how the public realm of this central area could be enhanced and woven together to form a coherent pedestrian realm.

Central to the scheme was our proposal to re-route traffic on the Embankment in order to create a new riverside park stretching from Parliament to Blackfriars where pedestrians could fully enjoy the Thames. This would consolidate London's finest riverside and its existing mature gardens, creating a sweeping two-kilometre linear park – the first great park since the nineteenth century. The park could spill out onto the river: moored ships, pontoons and boardwalks could link the many monuments and sights of London, extending the public domain onto the river and creating new views. This project remains on the drawing board.

Trafalgar Square is now little more than the centre of a roundabout: tourists arc disappointed by it, Londoners ignore it. But the square could regain its civic importance by the pedestrianising of the road which cuts it off the from the National Gallery. This could be done tomorrow by redirecting the traffic flow at the top of Whitehall. The former road could become a new terrace for public sculpture, and the square would be liberated for the rest of London. Trafalgar Square itself could be remodelled to accommodate cafés and activities in an arcade tucked below the existing terrace. The result would be a vibrant meeting place for Londoners and a place to enjoy outstanding views of the turrets, domes and towers of Whitehall and the Palace of Westminster. Ten years after our original proposals, the idea was

London as it Could Be, 1986
Richard Rogers Partnership

▲ Plan showing the proposed car-free pedestrian realm.

▲ Sketch of the proposed replacement for Hungerford Railway Bridge.

▶ Aerial view of central London.
Aerofilms

London as it Could Be, 1986
Richard Rogers Partnership

▲ Sketch of the proposed pedestrianisation of the Embankment in front of Somerset House.

◄ Pedestrianising the Embankment Road creates the opportunity to link the existing historic gardens into a mile-long linear park stretching from Westminster to Blackfriars Bridge.
Eamonn O'Mahony

► Proposed replacement for Hungerford Railway Bridge designed to break the division between North and South Banks. A single-span pedestrian bridge with underslung shuttle linking the suggested North Embankment Linear Park to the heart of the South Bank Centre, and inhabiting the river with floating restaurants and facilities.
Richard Davies

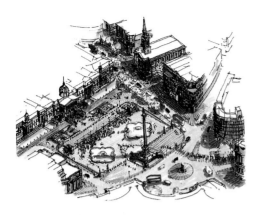

London as it Could Be, 1986
Richard Rogers Partnership

Meeting places for people

◀ View of the proposed pedestrianisation of Trafalgar Square showing traffic re-routed to the south.

▼ View of the proposed 'reclaimed' terrace fronting the National Gallery: a new open-air sculpture space for London.

finally taken up by the Minister of the Environment, John Gummer, who commissioned a study of the area from Trafalgar Square to Parliament Square with a view to planning a programme of pedestrianisation.

We should be radical in approach and continue to challenge tradition. The entire arcade of the Mall, which houses among other buildings the Institute of Contemporary Arts and which at present is restricted from spilling out onto the generous pavement area, should be opened onto St James's Park. This would create a beautiful and animated walk between Trafalgar Square and Buckingham Palace.

Albertopolis in South Kensington is one of the greatest collections of museums and universities in the world, ranging from the Royal Colleges of Art and of Music to the Natural History Museum, the Victoria & Albert Museum and the Science Museum. It is the enduring legacy of a far-sighted Prince, but it lacks a public domain and therefore fails to develop into the exciting cultural district it could be. Its present disorder warrants the demolition of the worst buildings in order to create a coherent public space. An underpass between the Albert Hall and the Albert Memorial would connect Albertopolis with Kensington Gardens and create a natural meeting place for the thousands of visitors who attend events at the Hall. This link would also draw people from the park towards the exhibition spaces and concert halls that fill the site. The pedestrianisation of Exhibition Road would in effect extend Hyde Park into the heart of the museums' site, linking directly to South Kensington Station. In this way what is currently a desolate area in terms of public life could be transformed into a vibrant daytime and evening cultural quarter.

These examples focus on London's national centres, but the same process could take place in local centres like Shepherd's Bush, Brixton and the Elephant & Castle. Re-routing, burying or

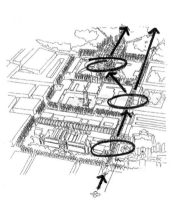

Albertopolis
Richard Rogers Partnership

▲ Proposals to pedestrianise Exhibition Road and create a tree-lined avenue linking Kensington to the museum site and on to the park.

Park or play?

◀ Typical residential street overwhelmed by cars. Rainville Road, London.
Emma England

▼ Street grassed over for a day, Leeds.
Ross–Parry Agency

pedestrianising roads could liberate unused public spaces throughout London. A map of London shows its great heritage of magnificent public spaces and local parks. Along with these planned elements are the informal, unplanned but equally popular places. Today these spaces are isolated one from the other. We need to link them together along the quieter routes with pedestrian and cycle paths. Where no links exist, we could use the canal tow paths, open up squares, landscape abandoned railway lines or simply calm traffic and pedestrianise roads. It would not be hard, for instance, to create continuous cycle routes from Richmond Park to Greenwich and from Highgate to Clapham Common, with new pedestrian bridges across the Thames. A million trees could be planted to celebrate the millennium, marking 'green routes' for pedestrians and cyclists across London; the trees would not only beautify the city but would also reduce noise and absorb carbon dioxide. All these spaces could be regained for people – outdoor living rooms for London's communities – and could be achieved by implementing a series of local projects rather than sweeping Beaux Arts masterplans.

Look at any satellite image of the capital: it is the Thames that dominates. Historically, the river is the very reason for London's existence. Once a thriving commercial highway serving the heart of the city, today it lies deserted, its presence in the city insignificant. The Thames, alongside which so many of Britain's greatest political, religious, commercial and cultural institutions grew up, is now merely a divisive element separating the poorer south of London from the more prosperous north. It is this beautiful waterway bordering nineteen of London's boroughs which holds the key to revitalising the spirit of the metropolis. If we redefine our use and perception of the river it could once again link communities.

The Thames is one of the broadest rivers to bisect a capital city, and its broadness exaggerates its divisiveness. London needs many

Only connect

▲ Forging pedestrian and cyclist links between existing centres creates a coherent public realm that encourages walking and cycling.
Richard Rogers Partnership

more bridges if it is to break this sense of separation. Central Paris, for example, has three times the number of bridges. And yet a well-designed single span bridge for pedestrians and cyclists costs only around £7 million. The City of London Corporation is proposing to build a new footbridge linking St Paul's to Bankside. Where the pedestrian flow is likely to be substantial, inhabited bridges similar to the old London Bridge could be constructed.

Pedestrian and public transport routes of all types are also needed to connect the centres of boroughs to the river. A new tram route has been proposed to link Waterloo Station across the Thames to the new British Library. The architects Michael and Patti Hopkins have proposed a cable-car route that begins in Covent Garden, passes over the linear park described above, and terminates on the South Bank. The architect Will Alsop has proposed a new Institute of Contemporary Arts building spanning the river at Blackfriars.

My own practice is proposing a route linking Trafalgar Square to Waterloo Station. The pedestrianised Trafalgar Square would be linked to a semi-pedestrianised Northumberland Avenue, and the Thames crossed by a new bridge with restaurants and cafés. This bridge would act as a square: suspended above the Thames, it would enjoy the most spectacular views of the Palace of Westminster and break the isolation of the south bank at this point.

The stretch of the river from Westminster Bridge to Tower Bridge is the most glaring example of unexploited opportunity. On its banks are located some of our most famous buildings and some of our most important cultural institutions – from the Houses of Parliament to the Tower of London, from Tower Bridge to the Festival Hall and from Southwark Cathedral to Westminster Abbey. It is also less than 500 metres from Covent Garden, St Paul's, the Strand, the Old Vic and the brilliant new Eurostar station by Nicholas Grimshaw at

Expanding public realm

▲ View of the Thames from Tower Bridge towards the West End.
Aerofilms

▲ As it is: the River Thames from Westminster Bridge to Tower Bridge showing areas of intense public activity.

▶ As it will be: when the new lottery-funded cultural projects will spearhead the development of one of Europe's newest cultural districts. Grey areas show intensity of public activities. The South Bank redevelopment will revitalise two of London's poorest boroughs.

Richard Rogers Partnership

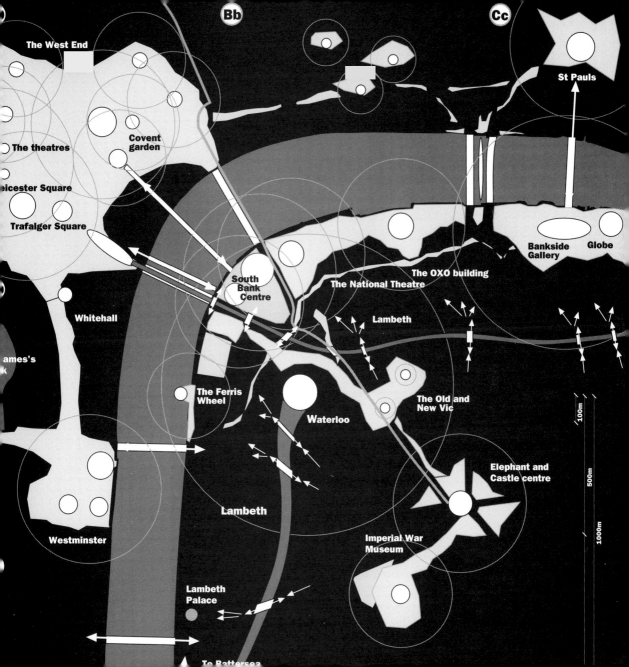

Waterloo, although we seldom associate such places with the river. Yet this section of the Thames, at the very centre of the nation's capital, remains wastefully underused.

The lack of a riverside road and the availability of sites for redevelopment makes the South Bank an ideal area for transformation into a vibrant cultural district that could regenerate the areas around it. Much of the South Bank is already undergoing radical transformation: the new Shakespeare Centre, the new Tate Museum of Modern Art at Bankside, broad-ranging projects in Southwark, community development on Coin Street, the Millennium Ferris wheel and a new aquarium at County Hall.

At the heart of the South Bank, on the bend of the river, lies Europe's largest cultural centre that includes concert halls, museums and cinemas. In 1995 our practice won the commission to revitalise and greatly expand the use and diversity of activities of the centre, with the aim of more than doubling the number of visitors. The project consists of three distinct strategies: first, construction of a large undulating crystal canopy extending over existing buildings and public spaces; second, giving all the ground level now used as service yards back to the people; third, creating new events and new facilities. Together these elements will generate a vibrant twenty-four-hour cultural destination which will draw an expected 3 million visitors to the area. The glass structure raises the temperature of the open public spaces below it: a 3°C increase could give a climate similar to Bordeaux, making this stretch of the riverside usable throughout the year.

The Thames must once more become the heart of the capital and a means of contact and communication rather than of separation. Once centres of activity along its banks are established and thriving, demand will follow for travel from one riverside node to another.

South Bank Redevelopment
Richard Rogers Partnership

▲ Computer-rendered drawing of the proposed Crystal Roof over the Hayward Gallery, Purcell Room and Queen Elizabeth Hall which will create a covered meeting place with cafés, restaurants, bookshops and galleries. The glass roof over the South Bank Centre ameliorates climate and extends the usable area to create a year-round people's place, and allows for tripling the number of visitors.
Hayes Davidson

▶ Conceptual sketch, 1994.

Thames Millennium Map

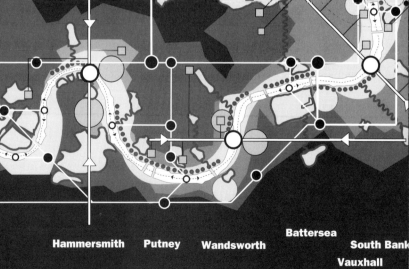

KEY

⬤ River Node

◯— Underground / BR station

• River pier

■ Event

Parks

⌇⌇⌇⌇ Green paths

••••• New parks

Site (exhibitions, events, festivals)

Hinterland

Kew

Hammersmith Putney Wandsworth

Battersea

South Bank

Vauxhall

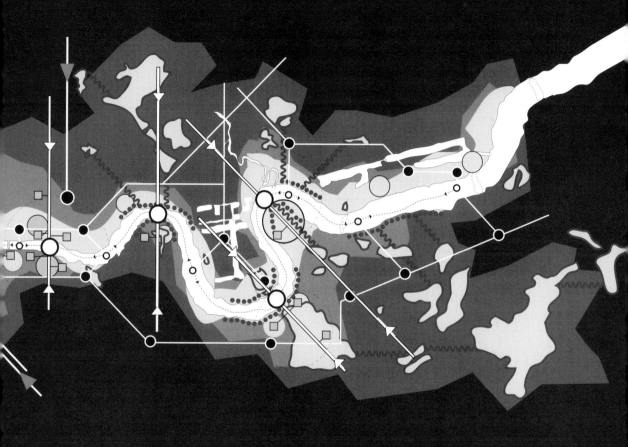

Tower Bridge   **Greenwich**   **Woolwich**

A riverbus system can be built for a fraction of the cost of a conventional fixed transport system. Riverbus piers should be developed in each of the nineteen boroughs bordering the Thames to form a coherent network of piers from Kew to Greenwich. These should be fine pieces of architecture; they would integrate the riverbus system into the overall transport network and would also function as important commercial hubs, reinforcing the economic and social activity of their areas. Together, bridges and riverbus piers could become economic and social magnets central to the lives of their boroughs, capable of stimulating new development on the many derelict riverside sites and over time creating a series of river-based compact urban centres.

None of the above projects is beyond our means, and they could all be brought into existence sooner rather than later – for the approach of the millennium is providing London with a once-in-a-lifetime opportunity. We have for the first time in generations the chance to generate a sufficient critical mass of architectural projects, festivals, exhibitions and celebrations to re introduce the Thames into the lives of Londoners.

National Lottery awards will be made to the National Millennium Exhibition, marking the time/space start of the third millennium on the Greenwich meridian, and to architectural projects throughout the capital. The challenge is to make these projects contribute to a new vision for London, to make the whole greater than the sum of its parts. With its immense cultural, political and social resources, London could become the city to visit in the year 2000. It should host a year-long millennium celebration of unrivalled quality and diversity at Greenwich and throughout the capital.

If the Seville Expo of 1992 was able to draw 46 million visits in eight months, one would expect London's millennium celebration to draw

▲ *previous page*
Millennium Map, 1996
Richard Rogers Partnership

Refocusing London on the Thames will in turn regenerate the 19 riparian Boroughs.

Plan showing an accumulation of small projects and pedestrianisation initiatives that could refocus London onto its great River Thames. River bus piers linked into the overall public transport network form the heart of densely developed riverside nodes. From these, links across the river and into the hinterland forge city to river.

River transport could be the main transportation for a London-wide Millennium Festival taking place in its major public spaces, cultural and religious institutions and at the main National Exhibition site at Greenwich. This approach would create a sufficient critical mass of small-scale projects to weave the Thames back into the lives of Londoners.

many more. If we embrace this idea, we will need to improve the city's public transport and pedestrian routes to cope with the extra visitors. Lottery funds should be used strategically to spearhead this transformation of the city. The Thames provides a perfect highway to carry visitors between the events: a necklace stringing together all the activities along the river, with extensions reaching out to the public spaces beyond. The National Millennium Exhibition at Greenwich would serve as the clasp of the necklace.

The riverbus would bring the festival to the furthest boroughs of London. Specially designed for the Thames and carrying the latest technology to supply event information in many languages, riverbuses could be events in themselves. Going to the festival would simply entail going to your nearest pier and selecting your destination while you sail. By making events and sites more accessible, riverbuses could free tourists from dependence on organised tours; tourism would be redefined for both Britons and foreigners, and visiting London would become a far more interactive and personal experience.

This approach to celebrating the millennium would leave a functioning riverbus service and riverbanks revitalised with parks, promenades, piers, floating restaurants and boardwalks. The Thames restored to the people and the linking of London's public spaces should be the physical legacy of the city's millennium celebrations – a thriving public domain that strings together our national monuments and places, past and future.

London has the opportunity to become a cultured, balanced and sustainable city. It is up to Londoners to demand an elected strategic body to deliver its full potential.

5   Cities for a small planet

The Atom is the past. The symbol of science for the next century is the dynamical Net. The Net is the archetype displayed to represent all circuits, all intelligence, all interdependence, all things economic and social and ecological, all communications, all democracy, all groups, all large systems.

Kevin Kelly,
Out of Control

5 The dissemination of knowledge about the global crisis has generated world-wide recognition that our environment is a fragile and limited asset. Just as new technical knowledge transformed the agrarian village into the industrial society, so information technology, carrying with it new environmental knowledge, is forcing the creation of a global society – a society that recognises the need to be supremely mindful of the environmental and social consequences of its actions.

Micro-electronics and the information network are at the core of this transformation, and not simply because they have helped bring the global perspective into view or facilitated new and more powerful technologies. Communication technologies are transforming our economies, our ways of learning, our methods of work, our capacity to alter the environment and even our daily chores and pleasures; they are unmistakably reshaping our lives. But they are also at the core of a fundamental new gearing of the human mind.

New technologies are enabling us to expand the use of our most valuable and most particularly human resource: creative imagination, or brain power. The increased or even prolific consumption of this resource is subject to no limiting factors and has no downside; it is people- and environment-friendly. Whereas industrial wealth depended on solid matter like coal and iron, the sustainable wealth on which the post-industrial society will depend is grey matter.

'It is unarguably true that there are only two primary sources of wealth available to us: what we get from the earth itself and what we get from our own creative imaginations. Unless we start relying less on the former and much more on the latter, then it is inconceivable that we can sustain the growing population of the world with anything approaching decent, civilised and broadly comparable standards of living.' (David Puttnam)

▲ *previous page*
Cyber-City

Far from becoming obsolete, cities are centres for concentrations of vast networks of computerised information. Silicone chip. *Integrated Circuit*
Erich Hartmann, Magnum

It is in this context that the role of technology is paramount. Micro-electronics are producing a step-change in our ability to network people, their knowledge and their brain power – we are experiencing a period of social revolution as significant as that engendered by the invention of Caxton's printing press or the telegraph. The potential of the individual brain is about to be expanded unquantifiably by the networking of thinking.

But the concept of network also offers advantages at the macro scale. It has the potential to replace our exclusive and linear models of planning and analysis with participatory and multi-dimensional ones. The Net, just like the Swarm, offers a structure of simultaneous possibilities. It is resilient, evolvable and boundless, ideal for supreme adaptability. As a system it is ultimately inclusive, encompassing, as Kevin Kelly describes it, small failures in order that large failures do not happen. It generates control without authority. It embraces complexity.

It is my hope that this technological invention will play a central role in the tempering of our destructive potential. It is a tool that offers the possibility of creating infinite and sustainable wealth. We are at the threshold of a new interaction of people, knowledge and the environment and the global city is at the heart of this new spatial and economic order – the powerhouse at the centre of this web of knowledge.

In this technological age, problems and opportunities abound in equal measure. On the positive side, robotics and electronics are replacing physically exhausting and repetitive work practices. Working conditions have radically improved and the 80-hour week of a hundred years ago has given way to the 37-hour week of present times. In the same period medical innovation and technology have more than doubled the average life expectancy to eighty years, and

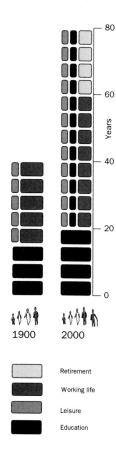

80

60

Years

40

20

0

👤👤👤👤   👤👤👤👤👤
1900   2000

Retirement

Working life

Leisure

Education

Changing life patterns

▲ As life-span expectations
increase, so work and
parenting decrease
proportionately as the main
preoccupations of our adult
lives. This leaves a significant
proportion of our lives for non-
vocational work: potential time
for creative citizenship.

it is expected to increase further. People born today can reasonably look forward to living for over 100 years.

For the first time since the industrial revolution the greater part of human activity need not be dominated by either employment or parenthood. Rather, work and parenthood have become 'intervals' in a long life. Statistically, work now occupies under one third of an adult's working life, which itself occupies on average only half of an individual's lifespan. This leaves an average twenty years of retirement. The period spent 'parenting' has also dropped as a percentage of total lifespan. These trends are leaving the greater part of one's time under-employed or retired – time available for non-vocational, free-time activities.

But while these developments bring huge opportunities, they also engender considerable challenges and social costs – most notable amongst them, unemployment. Robotisation is replacing not only laborious work but also the workers themselves. Life without work can lack purpose, and living in the consumer society without the wealth derived from work is decidedly alienating. Some unions and businesses (such as Volkswagen and Hewlett-Packard) are attempting to share the limited amount of available work by reducing the working week yet further. Ironically, we have gone from too much work to too little.

A person's life is now less defined by skill, craft or profession; it is also less defined by religion and less guided by the close community. In many countries the young are faced with the prospect of permanent unemployment from the day they leave school. We see the despair of those without work, or without adequate means, in the increasing retreat into drug abuse or in anger vented against society in the vandalising of buildings and the burning of cities.

The politicians' response is more pious words about parental control without thought to the causes of today's rebellions. They call for greater discipline, more security, tougher prison sentences, and this is followed by surprise when ex-prisoners re-offend. We are faced with a fragmentation of our society, the breakdown of our communities and families. An unstable social environment is being created, and all that is offered to fill the vacuum of people's lives is TV.

Bold innovations are needed if we are to resolve this crisis. In this chapter I want to explore how changing our understanding of the role of urban culture, how reforming our economic systems and our mechanisms of government, could lead to a sustainable future; and I will speculate on what that future would be like.

We have never before been linked more closely electronically and physically, yet never before have we been more socially separated. Individual freedom has reduced our interdependence and as a consequence our sense of common interest. To counterbalance these forces we need to encourage and properly reward participation in those occupations which underpin society. We could harness the potential of the 'free time' afforded by the new technological age by extending the concept of 'work' to include a broader range of cultural activity – work in families, citizens' advice groups, civil rights, youth organisations, health care, the environment, the arts and life-long education. This 'work' – a form of creative citizenship – would address social needs which the market system overlooks and would nurture qualities that humanise and inspire lives.

'Creative citizenship' is participation in essentially creative communal activities. It could animate communities; it could fill a vacuum in many lives now empty of purpose; it could provide status, satisfaction and identity, and begin to tackle the cause of much of society's disharmony and alienation. It could also generate the basis for a more creative and motivated workforce.

'Think of society as a three-legged stool made up of the market sector, the government sector and the civil sector. The first leg creates market capital, the second leg creates public capital and the third leg creates social capital.' (Jeremy Rifkin, *The Environment of Work*)

In the long term, the social, environmental and economic benefits of this type of civil employment could transform patterns of urban life. We have viewed the development of our cities as the responsibility of the public and private sectors alone. The post-industrial city now requires the participation of the civil sector. Deploying the energy of dispossessed labour, the underused skills of youth and the experience of age on tackling the problems ignored by a dwindling public sector and a profit-driven private sector will result in replacing poverty, dependence and alienation with equity, initiative and participation.

Environmental initiatives, education, even audiences generate social wealth. If we begin to see all these activities as productive work, a concept of a creative society emerges. In a creative society every unemployed citizen should have the right to civil employment. Society as a whole gains from creative citizenship because it generates social wealth.

The shape of the city can encourage an urban culture that generates citizenship. This important role needs to be recognised. To my thinking urban culture is fundamentally participatory. It manifests itself in activities that take place only in the dense and interactive environment of towns and cities. These range from the ordinary to the high-brow, from the everyday to the exceptional, from the amusing to the profound. From heated exchanges of views in cafés to listening to Birtwistle in a concert hall, these activities define the character of a particular city, they give identity to an urban society, capture the essence of its people and bind the community.

5
151

Culture is the soul of that society and the quality that struggles against repression. It differentiates people in this age of globalisation and sameness.

I have spoken about a city's positive ability to encourage this rich interaction and also of its damaging capacity to stifle it. The public domain plays a crucial role in encouraging urban culture and creating citizenship. By public domain I am referring not only to the major urban spaces such as Piazza San Marco in Venice or the Garibaldi in Mexico City. These places have important social and symbolic functions, but they are simply the summit of a hierarchy of spaces that starts with the local street, the link from home to school, from shops to work.

Safe and inclusive public space, in all its forms from grand to intimate, is critical for social integration and cohesion. Democracy finds its physical expression in the open-minded spaces of the public realm, in the quality of its street life. Central to this is the way its buildings contain or act as backdrop to the spontaneous and chaotic enactment of everyday life. We are perhaps the first generation committed to equal rights and are therefore faced with the challenge of creating a public domain that is truly inclusive and accessible to all – we must persevere with our attempts to evolve this institution to reflect our new age.

Human rights create the freedom of public space. Without them the public domain is a sham – think of events in Tiananmen Square. The free expression in urban space of a citizen's rights creates the experience of freedom and helps to protect and nurture those rights. The Greek agora constituted just such a spatial expression of social rights, albeit the rights of an exclusive class. The physical and intellectual accessibility of the public domain is a litmus test of society's values: inclusive and thriving public spaces foster tolerance and radical thought. It is no accident that under Fascist or similarly repressive regimes the city is segregated and specifically designed to overwhelm the individual. Sharing public spaces breaks down prejudice and forces us to acknowledge common responsibilities. It binds communities.

Freedom of public space must be defended just as fiercely as freedom of expression. We need to recognise that the public domain includes our semi-private institutions – schools, universities, town halls, shopping centres – and ensure that these spaces are accessible to all and designed to the highest standards. The encroachment of private control demands public accountability: if the civic high street, for example, is replaced by a private shopping mall, the developers must satisfy the social needs of all the community. The freedom of cyberspace also must be included in our definition of the public domain and safeguarded as a public forum; it too can help create a community of equals.

At present we are building cities that segregate and brutalise rather than emancipate and civilise. But the recent revolution in our attitudes towards the natural environment provide a useful model. Ecologists' description of our relationship with nature – we are not its owners but its trustees, and have responsibilities towards future generations – applies just as well to the public life of cities. We are getting used to thinking about nature as being of ultimate value; we now need to think of the public domain in much the same way and invest in our citizens' public lives and public spaces.

How will the sustainable city emerge? Economics are inescapably at the heart of achieving sustainability, and we have a duty to examine the basic assumptions at the core of our economic thinking. Since the advent of industrialisation the emphasis has been on resource 'extraction and consumption'. Over the past two hundred years this has created highly efficient techniques and technologies hell-bent on a path of linear consumption and waste. The emphasis on GNP and GDP suggests that economic growth, *per se*, is a benefit but it fails to factor long-term criteria such as the fertility of the environment or the well being of society. If we sought a conceptual shift towards resource 'conservation and recycling', we can anticipate the market responding, in time, with equal voracity and efficiency. But how can this shift be achieved?

The current market approach is based on pricing goods by their cost of production, without factoring the impact of their use. Take the case of petrol. In the USA and many other countries petrol is actually cheaper than mineral water, although the consumption of petrol results in air pollution, ill health and the erosion of the land's fertility. Our wasteful ways of living are carried on the back of cheap petrol. The price? Massive long-term environmental damage, air pollution and medical costs for those affected by poor air and congested environments. In a single year we consume millions of years of our planet's stored energy, and at the same time fatally damage humankind's life support system. We are consuming future generations' wealth today.

Nor is the market alone in its damaging behaviour. A recent report from the Worldwatch Institute in Washington DC revealed that governments of the Western world were themselves responsible for over $500 billion of public expenditure that directly harms the environment. Bringing the activities of the market and the public sector into the complex matrix of sustainable accounting is desperately needed if we are to progress towards sustainable living, a fact which is now publicly recognised:

'For development to be sustainable, environmental considerations must become a central part of the decision-making process within government and industry. For this to happen, better information is

Gross Domestic Product
GDP is calculated by adding all activities together, including those which reduce the quality of life.

Index of Sustainable Economic Wealth
ISEW on the other hand takes account of negative costs, and includes some social factors which GDP ignores.

GDP is no longer an appropriate means of judging the standards of living. Issues such as pollution, waste, health and security need to be factored into the equation.
Richard Rogers Partnership/ New Economics Foundation

needed on the way in which economic development impacts on the environment. The ultimate goal would be the integration of environmental and economic accounting in national accounts.'
(UK Government White Paper, January 1994)

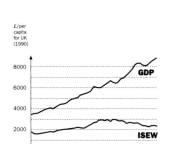

£/per
capita
for UK
(1990)

Graph showing the widening gap between GDP and quality indicators such as ISEW.

There is an imperative need for a new concept of holistic economic evaluation. Sustainability can be seen as a measure of efficiency, but one defined by complex, broad, long-term criteria rather than simple, narrow, short-term ones. Sustainability is thus a higher order of economic efficiency, and one that benefits all, rather than few to the detriment of the many.

The market is responsive, flexible and, within short-term criteria, highly efficient, but we must feed into the economic equation long-term environmental and social factors. Proponents of sustainability such as David Pearce, Professor of Economics at London University, claim that the market can be managed by government so that short-term 'efficiency' can be generated without incurring ecological and social 'inefficiencies'.

Governments should impose environmental levies or 'green' taxes on activities that damage the environment, reflecting external costs in the purchase price of goods. This would manage market forces towards greener production solutions and marry the advantages of the market's responsiveness and ability to produce efficiency with the achievement of sustainability.

Apply this to fuel. Since the collapse of OPEC in 1986 the price of petrol has returned to its low pre-oil crisis level. Improvements in fuel economy in the vehicle sector that evolved post 1973 have gone into reverse. Many vehicle owners, encouraged by low petrol prices, are now choosing larger, heavier cars with more powerful engines. Tax-created price increases would quickly discourage consumers from buying energy-guzzling vehicles and would encourage manufacturers to implement the technological innovations that can reduce fuel consumption and pollution.

At present, taxation is seen mainly as a way of raising revenue rather than a tool that can influence corporate and individual behaviour. Taxation is set at the levels deemed tolerable by the market and the electorate. Thus the tax on fuel or vehicles is determined by the wish to maximise revenue without disrupting the economic status quo rather than by environmental or social considerations.

Environmental policies that encourage greater 'resource productivity' – more recycling and less waste – can produce virtuous circles. They tend to be more labour intensive and are predicted to generate large-scale urban job and business opportunities. This is quite logical: the shift from waste disposal by dumping at sea, burning or landfill, for example, to reprocessing and recycling demands a greater level of care. Resource productivity can be further encouraged by balancing taxation between people and machines. Government taxation policies generally favour 'mechanisation' as a means of increasing production. As a result they tend to subsidise automation by creating taxation structures that encourage 'tooling up' and discourage labour-intensive processes, giving tax breaks for investment in technology while continuing to raise revenue from labour. However, the assumption in favour of machine as against less 'productive' labour can be flawed: in some cases the employment of a person leads to broad social or environmental gains that far outweigh the apparent efficiency of the machine.

Take the apparently straightforward case of the London bus conductor – now close to extinction. Since rationalisation and privatisation of the bus routes and the 'efficiency' drive that followed, the duties of the conductor were taken on by the driver. Bus companies notionally doubled their productivity overnight by running the same line with half the numbers of staff and a little more equipment.

But what looks good on paper ignores the full economic, social and environmental impact of the change: buses that dally at bus stops (choking the air with fumes, lengthening journey times and slowing traffic behind them); no assistance for the disabled, the elderly, the tourist; no familiar face for young children; less feeling of security and less animation created by the presence of the often 'characterful' conductor; no sense of ownership of the passenger compartment – not to mention a few hundred unemployed bus conductors. We are given evidence that the buses are now run cheaper and that profits from re-sale are being shared with the remaining employees and managers, but there is no evidence that these changes have improved the overall public transport network or that more people are using the bus service more frequently. The costs – in wasted time, wasted fuel, congestion, pollution and unemployment – are picked up by society. The savings gained by society from this particular increase in productivity are an illusion.

And this example represents just the tip of the iceberg. The huge 'efficiencies' created by the multinationals who control some 50 per cent of all income mask the social as well as the environmental footprints of consumerist cities. A recent article in the *Guardian* described how the Philippines were aiming at turning themselves into an Asian Tiger on the back of an agricultural modernisation programme. Vast fruit plantations are replacing smallholdings, and multinationals are making them increasingly capital-intensive. Machines are replacing cutters, who now migrate to cities and well their shanty towns. Land previously used for cultivating maize and rice for the domestic market is being forced by comparatively low domestic prices to switch to luxury export crops for the industrial world. The land devoted to cultivating maize and rice is now predicted to shrink by half within a few years. True, the cost of a Philippine pineapple on a table in Paris, London, New York or Tokyo is highly competitive, but at what social cost along the way?

The extent to which these new 'efficiencies' create costs for society both at home and abroad should be carefully evaluated. Where society incurs costs, profits should be shared with social and educational programmes and not just distributed to shareholders and managers. As robotisation is taking over from the worker because it is better at creating certain types of wealth, so taxation must shift from the worker to the product. The ideal is to create a taxation framework that encourages the efficient, environmentally and socially sustainable interaction of society, nature and machine.

Governments should make the purpose of sustainability taxes transparent. In some cases, earmarking the revenue from green taxes for specific sustainability projects makes them more acceptable to the citizen: for example, using the revenue from raising the tax on petrol to improve public transport. Social security benefits should, where possible, be seen to be financing 'creative citizenship' initiatives that themselves create further social wealth rather than maintaining people in a state of dependency.

Land taxation should be designed to encourage urban consolidation rather than urban sprawl. At present some land taxes and public works actually promote urban sprawl and, as a consequence, inner-city dereliction and social decay. For example, publicly financed roads have transformed low-value agricultural land into accessible and valuable commercial property. Land taxes on developments on out-of-town sites should reflect the cost of publicly financed infrastructure and the costs to society of retail and commerce abandoning the inner city. This will increase the relative competitiveness of compact urban sites and will encourage developers and retailers to consolidate city centres. Applications for development should be accompanied by rigorous studies of their social and environmental impact. Taxes should penalise schemes that generate unacceptable levels of social segregation, congestion or pollution.

Progress towards sustainability requires reforming the structure of government itself. Today, governments still operate through ministries with individual agendas and without an overarching environmental or social strategy; these agendas are often incompatible with those of other ministries. Allowing department policies to pull in different directions is completely out of step with the demands of modern urban life. In Britain, for example, the Departments of Transport and of Trade and Industry have traditionally seen it as their responsibility to promote car use, while the departments of Environment and of Health have seen theirs as curbing it. We need holistic government structures which recognise the complexity of the modern city.

A bold step was taken in 1992 when the French government set up its Ministère des Villes to tackle the overlapping needs of its poorest citizens. Most of these live in deprived housing estates and suffer from the classic symptoms of poverty: bad education, bad environment and bad health, as well as high rates of crime, unemployment, drug abuse and social isolation. The previous structure had meant that each government ministry could only react to the effects of poverty and not actively address its causes. The job of the new Ministère des Villes was to co-ordinate the activities of the traditional ministries, creating an atmosphere in which they networked their resources and shared responsibility for the living conditions of disadvantaged citizens.

This sort of approach to planning for a sustainable environment, so clearly proven to be advantageous in cities such as Curitiba, will need to underpin future government policy. Many countries are beginning the process by introducing legislation that cuts across traditional boundaries of responsibilities. Most Western governments are beginning to apply the environmental principle of 'the polluter pays'. The German government, for instance, has passed new laws targeting domestic waste: the Materials Recirculation Law makes industrial producers responsible for the disposal of the products they manufacture – a responsibility normally falling on the end-user or the local authority. This type of law will have a dramatic effect on the attitudes of manufacturers towards packaging and recycling, and will begin to close the loop between production and consumption, rapidly improving the efficiency of the city's metabolism.

Good public information is essential if environmental policies are to be implemented and properly policed. Governments that have committed themselves to ecological targets must suffer penalties if these targets are not reached. Self-policing is vital. The UK, for example, has committed itself to complying with the WHO standards for ozone pollution by the year 2000; but, having made this commitment, it has repeatedly failed even to report those occasions when ozone levels have exceeded the standards.

Citizens will be able to apply real pressure on their governments if agreed international standards for measuring the environmental performance of cities are established, targets for improvements set and their progress monitored and publicly published. If this information is made publicly available through the Internet a clear and accessible global picture will emerge. International penalties and aid could be targeted at nations whose cities are failing sustainability criteria.

Governments must ensure that their own enormous direct purchasing power benefits environmental and social sustainability. Government procurement policies could promote innovation in all areas of sustainable design, from electric cars to low-energy buildings and inspiring educational environments.

For the last twenty-five years France has used its public building procurement budgets to commission quality public buildings as a means of increasing community, pride and cultural achievement.

This policy has been tremendously successful. It has raised public awareness of architecture and has led to countless good contemporary buildings throughout the country that have revitalised local communities. France's new buildings and parks have attracted enormous international acclaim and boosted tourism. France's architectural profession, which in the sixties and seventies enjoyed little international acclaim, is today universally admired, with innovative young architects and planners like Jean Nouvel, Dominique Perrault and Christian de Portzampark. Mitterrand's cultural programme produced a dynamic atmosphere and an open-minded attitude to the future.

Governments can ensure that they procure quality urban projects, encouraging innovation and experimentation. Simply by acting as informed patrons of architecture, ministers can set national standards for quality in the environment. Citizens have the right to expect their government to procure public buildings of the best architectural quality because they are so crucial to our everyday lives: architecture is the physical expression of an urban society's cultural development and social concerns. Governments could directly improve the quality of the environment and of the professions by seeking out the young, talented and imaginative, and encouraging them to work on our schools, hospitals and public housing.

Where there used to be two major economic partners – business and national governments – there is now a third: global cities. The information technologies that have made the global economy possible have created intense communication networks centred on the city. Firms that operate globally depend on the service infrastructures and skilled human resources that exist only in cities. This has concentrated massive resources in urban areas and created the new network of global cities. The transfer of economic power to cities has also been accompanied by the transfer of public services from government control to city control. The cities have become major economic and political powerhouses, and as technopoles they are the primary means by which nations interface with the global economy.

'Rather than becoming obsolete because of the dispersal made possible by information technologies, cities concentrate command functions in the global economy.' (Saskia Sassen)

The new information technology is transforming the economy at all levels. Citizens' minds and sophisticated technologies are replacing raw materials and brawn. The networking of creativity is now driving the new 'creative' economy. Exchanges between art and technology – the exchange of ideas rather than of commodities – are becoming the life-blood of the new economy and of our future prosperity. These changes directly affect the shape of the city because the information superhighway, cheap computing power and sophisticated manufacturing robotics revolutionise work practices. New technology is liberating learning and work from their traditional locations. The clean-cut boundaries of yesterday's activities – the factory, the office, the university – are being replaced by networked, flexible connections to sources of information. People will increasingly use knowledge when they want it and not just where it is institutionalised: one will be able to plug in and participate whether at home, at the café or in the park. Learning, living and working will continuously overlap.

These innovations could spur the restructuring of the city along sustainable lines. The industrial city of the nineteenth century evolved around rail access or supplies of coal and steel. The city of the late twentieth century was planned and developed around zones of single activity. In the twenty-first century city the economy's reliance on small-scale employment and creative exchange will generate far more diverse and personal needs. Small companies are less dependent on large-scale accommodation and more on the city's infrastructure and local services. The shift of emphasis from large corporate operations to networks of small ones reduces the need for people to work in large, static groups and prompts the emergence of local workplaces scattered throughout the city, complemented by concentrations of formal and informal meeting-places. This process will have an important impact on the behaviour of the city. The huge rush-hour peaks into and out of the centres will gradually shift towards a more even distribution of mobility throughout the day and throughout the city. This will produce a greater dependence and more even and efficient use of urban transport. A finer and more diverse texture of city will increase demand for those cultural activities and civil services which overlap rather than segregate. These trends provide economic justifications for planning cities around compact and ecologically sustainable communities.

Doing business – presenting and exchanging ideas – is recognisably reverting to being both a social and economic activity. This blurring of the boundary between work and the rest of daily life will focus the city into more compact and mixed social nuclei, a precondition for urban sustainability. In a world where wealth is generated by the creativity of citizens and where innovation will be prompted by the unpredictable and the spontaneous, city authorities will need to develop new policies that sustain the competitiveness and productivity of their citizens. How can the design of cities encourage the creative economy? Companies that can locate anywhere they want will go where they can attract good people in good places. The new economy will flourish in cities that have the right mixture of public life, mobility, life-long education and accessible cultural facilities.

The impact of accelerating change on the physical form of the city is radical. Institutions have shorter and shorter lives – railway stations are converted into museums, power plants into art galleries, churches into night-clubs, warehouses into homes – and it is now commonplace to anticipate that a building will outlive the purpose for which it is built in a matter of a few years. Modern life can no longer be defined in the long term and consequently cannot be contained within a static order of symbolic buildings and spaces. The classical order of architectural symbolism is no longer relevant. The viewer is no longer able to read the functions of buildings: the church, the town hall, the palace, the market, the factory. Buildings no longer symbolise a static hierarchical order; instead, they have become flexible containers for use by a dynamic society. However, it is the arrangement of buildings in space – the network of the city as a whole – that has come to be the dominant reflection of modern urban society.

As traditional ways of living give way to the onslaught of modern life, change can be painful and accompanied by further problems. The giant city of Tokyo – where the work ethos dominates life, where zoning and exorbitant land values have banished homes hours away from downtown work – has seen cultural traditions shifting dramatically. Home life in the residential areas has been marginalised and left for Sundays. Downtown urban space is shaped to satisfy both business and the weekday domestic needs of the marooned workers. Residential and urban functions begin to meld into one another and the relationship between inside and outside has been revised, so that the city centre becomes the house. Eating, sleeping and bathing are now carried out downtown: the living room has been replaced by cafés, bars, clubs and karaoke establishments; the dining room and the kitchen by counter eateries and fast food restaurants; the bathroom by sports clubs, saunas and spas; and the bedroom by inns, hostels and love hotels. The downtown area has a twenty-four-hour vitality that is awesome to experience, but the rest of one of the world's largest metropolitan areas is soulless and chaotic. This is just one example of how the shape and functioning of a city is constantly revised and adapted. The complexity of the forces and the power of the market to monopolise change require the broadest vigilance from citizens and governments.

We must build cities for flexibility and openness, working with and not against the now inevitable process whereby cities are subject to constant change. As homes, schools, entertainment and work-places become less defined by their single function, one basic structure, linked to a common communication network, can accommodate learning, work and leisure. Aesthetics are all but freed from association with the function that the building encloses. The building system itself – its craftsmanship, responsiveness and beauty – is fast becoming the dominant criterion. The aesthetics of response, change and modulation have replaced the fixed order of architecture.

Architecture is changing in response to environmental demands and the development of new high-performance and bio-responsive materials. Le Corbusier described architecture as the 'masterly correct and magnificent play of masses brought together in light'. In the future, however, buildings will tend to dematerialise. It will be an age not of mass but of transparency and veils: of indeterminate, adaptable and floating structures that respond to daily changes in the environment and patterns of use. The buildings of the future – already foreshadowed by the work of Will Alsop, Future Systems, Zaha Hadid, Rem Koolhaas, Daniel Libeskind, Coop Himmerblau and Toyo Ito – will be less like the immutable classical temples of the past and more like moving, thinking, organic robots. This new architecture will change the character of the public domain. As structures become lighter, buildings will become more permeable and pedestrians will move through them rather than around them. The street and the park may be part of the building, or the building might hover above them. The architect Cedric Price once said that the main problem with cities is that the buildings get in the way. In the future, this will be less inevitable.

It is transport that will make or break the sustainability of a city. Compact mixed-use communities should be grouped round public transport hubs with the individual community planned around walking and cycling distances. Some metropolitan authorities are already taking a radical new look at transport in their cities. In Strasbourg, for example, the visionary mayor, Catherine Trautmann, has pursued radical transport policies. Private cars are now banned from the city centre; there is a state-of-the-art tram system, and mini-electric vehicles are available for rent by the hour, day or week. Canals are used for transportation and their banks turned into landscaped pedestrian routes criss-crossing the city. Curitiba in Brazil has also transformed public perceptions of the transport system by restricting key routes to buses only, by designing buses that load and unload their passengers like subway trains, and by commissioning space-age glass bus stations built to the highest specifications. As a result, bus travel is popular with everyone because it is perceived as safe, quick and smart.

Throughout the world mega-urban regions based on increasingly rapid and efficient mechanical transportation systems are forming. Trains can already travel at nearly 300 kilometres per hour, and soon the introduction of Magnet-levitation trains will double that speed. In Europe and Asia, the expanding network of international high speed trains is linking cities, reinforcing their importance as hubs of communication and providing corridors for new compact development.

The present polluting and obstructive automobile technology – the car – could be re-engineered to cause no damage to the environment. It could even become fully robotised: self-guided along urban expressways. Cars in the future will be 'clean', but it will be cheaper, faster and more fun to travel by public transport. The car will be seen as a minor component of a complex and flexible network of transport systems. Citizens will have access to a transport internet that will instantaneously analyse the entire network, map the fastest route across town and tell them when and where the closest vehicle will arrive. This will enable the citizen to get about faster, more often and to more places.

Given the will to create them, cities of the future could provide the foundation for a society in which everyone participates in health, security, inspiration and justice. New technology could be creatively exploited to give our cities a new lease of life: a more sociable, more beautiful and more exciting life, above all a life determined by its citizenry.

The concept of the sustainable city recognises that the city needs to meet our social, environmental, political and cultural objectives as well as our economic and physical ones. It is a dynamic organism as complex as the society itself and responsive enough to react swiftly to its changes. The sustainable city is a city of many facets:

– A Just City where justice, food, shelter, education, health and hope are fairly distributed and where all people participate in government;

– A Beautiful City, where art, architecture and landscape spark the imagination and move the spirit;

– A Creative City, where open-mindedness and experimentation mobilises the full potential of its human resources and allows a fast response to change;

– An Ecological City, which minimises its ecological impact, where landscape and built form are balanced and where buildings and infrastructures are safe and resource-efficient;

– A City of Easy Contact and Mobility, where information is exchanged both face-to-face and electronically;

– A Compact and Polycentric City, which protects the countryside, focuses and integrates communities within neighbourhoods and maximises proximity;

– A Diverse City, where a broad range of overlapping activities create animation, inspiration and foster a vital public life.

The sustainable city could be the agent for delivering environmental rights (basic rights to clean water, clean air, fertile land) to our new, dominantly urban, global civilisation. There are millions now and there will soon be billions who enjoy no such rights. Commitment to environmental rights demands the emergence of the sustainable city – in fact the two are interdependent. Take the issue of clean air or health. Currently millions of shanty dwellers are burning solid fuels to cook and warm themselves; this creates dangerous levels of air pollution from which they cannot escape. A city commited to human rights must provide clean energy, it must carry out policies that increase its efficiency and reduce its pollution. This in turn alleviates the global environmental crisis for all.

The world-wide environmental and social crisis of our cities has focused minds. The call for sustainability has revived the need for considered urban planning and has demanded a rethink of its basic principles and objectives. The crisis of modern civilisation demands that governments plan for sustainable cities.

The evidence indicates a shift towards the realisation of these ambitions. A world-wide trend is seeing power being devolved and shared between nations, international organisations and metropolitan authorities. The United Nations' Habitat Conference in 1996 brought these new relationships to the fore. For the first time national diplomats and ministers were faced with a coherent demand from city authorities to play a key part in the proceedings. Representatives of cities throughout the world presented proposals

The sustainable city is:

– A Just City, where justice, food, shelter, education, health and hope are fairly distributed and where all people participate in government;

– A Beautiful City, where art, architecture and landscape spark the imagination and move the spirit;

– A Creative City, where open-mindedness and experimentation mobilise the full potential of its human resources and allows a fast response to change;

– An Ecological City, which minimises its ecological impact, where landscape and built form are balanced and where buildings and infrastructures are safe and resource-efficient;

– A City of Easy Contact and Mobility, where information is exchanged both face-to-face and electronically;

– A Compact and Polycentric City, which protects the countryside, focuses and integrates communities within neighbourhoods and maximises proximity;

– A Diverse City, where a broad range of overlapping activities create animation, inspiration and foster a vital public life.

to Conference. Over and over again the plight of citizens, and particularly of developing world citizens, was exposed. The future of humanity was proved to be dependent on the quality of the city environment. The World Bank immediately replied with a threefold expansion of its grants to cities.

Urban planning is now recognised as being both interdisciplinary and no longer limited by metropolitan boundaries. Increasingly urban planners are considering the city, its neighbouring cities and its regional context. In many cases urban planning zones have been expanded into urban regions – for example, the Portland–Seattle–Vancouver axis, or the Amsterdam–Rotterdam axis – where cities, agriculture, economics and the environment are considered in parallel and planning is focused on strategic long-term objectives.

In Europe, cities such as Barcelona, Lyon and Glasgow are forging links with other dynamic cities and setting targets and implementing policies to improve the quality of urban life and limit the ecological impact of their cities. These policies, which often echo the ambitions of the European Union or international agreements such as the Rio proclamation, are often at odds with the short-term agendas of national governments. This is most notable when the issues of reduction of greenhouse gases, traffic or of investment in public transport are raised.

Network city

▶ Part of the global network of cities: Europe at night. *W. T. Sullivan and Hansen, Planetarium; Science Photo Library*

California provides another example of regional urban action. California defined different categories for low-emission vehicles and deadlines for these vehicles forming a percentage of total vehicle sales (by 2003, 10 per cent of all cars sold in the state are to be zero-emission vehicles). This action sent a clear message to manufacturers and initiated real research and development. As a direct result a General Motors electric car went on sale in California in 1996 and major improvements in vehicle emissions have been implemented.

City-based legislation could spur major technological and behavioural changes reaching far beyond the immediate city boundaries. Technical solutions already exist that can reduce the energy and resource use of a wide range of urban products. Vehicles, air-conditioners, refrigerators, packaging and distribution could be made far more environmentally friendly if cities set co-ordinated energy and recycling targets. These initiatives would boost development of new resource-productive technologies for all cities and are relevant to cities throughout the world whether rich or poor.

City power and participatory citizenship balance the ineffectiveness of national government to deal with the diversity and specificity of a city's problems. Greater city autonomy and greater participation by the citizen will create public policies targeted at the specific problem in the specific environment. The city's own government is best placed to decide on the requirements of its transport system, its social welfare, education and energy programmes. If the city is committed to sustainability then its citizens themselves are brought directly into a collaborative engagement with the global environmental crisis. The networking of cities creates a global network of interdependent citizens.

A major obstacle to our achievement of the goals I have defined is current trends in wealth disparity. The average per capita consumption of energy in the developed world today is six times higher than in developing countries, and the per person use of water is a hundred times larger. The United Nations Development Programme (UNDP) Human Development Report for 1992 reveals that the developed world, one-fifth of the world population, receives over 80 per cent of the world's income, sixty times that of the poorest fifth, who survive on less than 2 per cent. This gap has doubled since 1960. And this global trend is mirrored in the wealth differentials emerging within developed countries themselves. In the

USA by the early 1990s the share of wealth held by the top 1 per cent of the population was 40 per cent, double that of the 1970s and back to the levels of the 1920s, and this trend is as true in Britain. John Kavanagh of the Institute of Policy Research in Washington has calculated that the combined wealth of the world's 380 individual billionaires exceeds the combined annual income of half of the world's entire population.

Reports by the World Bank, the Organisation for Economic Co-operation and Development (OECD) and the UNDP have all condemned the rising tide of inequality. From observation around the world they have concluded that contrary to the market thinking of the 1980s, the inequality deliberately promoted by Thatcherism and Reaganomics as an aid to economic growth in fact hinders it. The failure of the 'trickle-down' theory is there for all to see in the desperate landscapes of world poverty.

These negative social trends are taking place in an environment where technological advances are consistently increasing wealth production faster than population growth. Since 1900 wealth production, measured by global GNP, has multiplied thirty-six-fold while in the same period the world's population has grown only five-fold. Michael Bruno of the World Bank has stated that reducing inequality not only benefits the poor immediately but benefits all through higher growth.

'Countries that give priority to basic human capabilities in schooling, health and nutrition not only directly enhance well being, but are also more likely to see improving income distribution and higher average incomes over the long term.' (The World Bank Report)

$\frac{5}{173}$

The determined and ecologically damaging pattern of economic growth of the developing world is causing an exponential increase in pollution. Demand for energy, water and resources is multiplying.

The UN has stated that some 1.3 billion have no access to clean water and has predicted that almost 3 billion people will be severely short of water within 50 years. The environmental crisis is about to be multiplied many times.

It is my contention that the developed world – with its disproportionate ownership of wealth, control of technology and influence over the means of production – bears an inescapable responsibility to make its own economies and cities sustainable. We must now implement real efficiencies that lower levels of consumption. How can a fairer distribution of resources be achieved?

Sustainability is about finding more socially cohesive, economically efficient and ecologically sound ways of producing and distributing existing resources. It is about securing quality of life by establishing the value of goods held in common – the environment and the community – and about recognising our mutual dependence on both. The planet is perfectly capable of sustaining all humanity if we respect the demands of nature and focus our use of technology.

'Science now finds there is ample for all, but only if the sovereign fences are completely removed. The basic you-or-me-not-enough-for-both-ergo-someone-must-die-tenets . . . are extinct.'
(Buckminster Fuller)

The dedicated application of sustainability in the developed world will lead to a dramatic reduction of the giant and damaging ecological footprints of the consumerist cities. It will set new international standards and pioneer the development of sustainable technologies. It will create the opportunity to distribute global wealth democratically and help the sprawling mega-cities of the developing world cope with the astounding demands of their own growth.

'Far from becoming a source of global environmental discord, environmentalism binds nations to a common concern, which will be the best thing that ever happened to international relations.'
(Greg Easterbrook)

Networks of cities across the world – sharing knowledge, technologies, services and recycled resources, and framing joint policies that both respect local cultures and implement common environmental objectives – could provide the structure and power to achieve real change. As the awareness of our common dependence on the global ecology spreads, and as modern communications bring the world's problems into sharper and more personal focus, there can be liaison, co-operation and support between first and third worlds. The expansion of cities' political power and recognition of their social and ecological responsibilities could radically reform international approaches to environmental issues. The magnitude of this task should not be underestimated, but nor should it deter positive action.

Our aim must be to achieve a new and dynamic equilibrium between society, cities and nature. Participation, education and innovation are the driving forces of the sustainable society.

Sustainable policies are already reaping visible rewards. On the back of this success and with popular determination sustainability could become the dominant philosophy of our age. In this way, cities, the habitat of humanity, could be once more woven into the cycle of nature.

Cities that are beautiful, safe and equitable are within our grasp.

Bibliography

Anson, Brian, *Don't Shoot the Graffiti Man*, unpublished works

Benevolo, Leonardo, *The European City*

Berman, Marshall, *All That is Solid Melts into Air: The Experience of Modernity*, Simon and Schuster 1982

Brotchie, John; Baffy, Michael; Hall, Peter and Newton, Peter (eds), *Cities of the 21st Century, New Technologies and Spatial Systems*, first edition, Longman 1991

Brown, Lester R. and others, *State of the World – A Worldwatch Institute Report on Progress Towards a Sustainable Society*, Earthscan Worldwatch Institute 1992

Carson, Rachel, *Silent Spring*, Houghton Mifflin Co. 1962

Castels, Manuel and Hall, Peter, *Technologies of the World – The Making of 21st Century Industrial Complexes*, Routledge 1994

Daton, Rio, *Researching the International Order*

Davies, Robert, *Death of the Streets – Cars and the Mythology of Road Safety*, Leading Edge Press and Publications Ltd 1992

Drucker, Peter F., *Post-Capitalist Society*, Butterworth Heinemann 1993

Easterbrook, Greg, *A Moment on the Earth*, Penguin 1995

Elkin, Tim; McLaren, Duncan and Hillman, Mayer, *Reviving the City – Towards Sustainable Urban Development*, Friends of the Earth 1991

Elkins, Paul; Hillman, Mayer and Hutchison, Robert, *Wealth Beyond Measure – Atlas of New Economics*, Gaia Books 1992

Freundt, Peter and Martin, George, *The Ecology of the Automobile*, Black Rose Ltd 1993

Galbraith, John Kenneth, *The New Industrial State*, first edition, Andre Deutsch 1972; second edition, Penguin Books 1991

Girardet, Herbert, *The Gaia Atlas of Cities*, Gaia Books 1992

Gore, Al, *Earth in the Balance – Ecology and the Human Spirit*, Penguin 1993

Gorz, André and Turner, Chris, *Capitalism, Socialism, Energy*, Verso

Hall Peter, *London 2001* and *Cities of Tomorrows*, Blackwell 1988

Harvey, David, *The Condition of Postmodernity*, Basil Blackwell 1989

International Institute for Environment and Development, *Policies for a Small Planet*, Earthscan Publishers 1992

Jacobs, Jane, *The Death and Life of Great American Cities – The Future of Town Planning*, first edition Penguin 1961; reprinted by Pelican Books 1965

Kelly, Kevin, *Out of Control*, Fourth Estate 1995

Kennedy, Paul, *Preparing for the 21st Century*, HarperCollins 1993

Kropotkin, Peter, *Mutual Aid – A Factor of Evolution*, Freedom Press 1993

Leggett, Jermey, *Global Warming – The Greenpeace Report*, Oxford University Press 1990

London City Council, *County of London Plan*, second printing, Macmillan and Co. 1943

Lovelock, James, *The Ages of Gaia*, Oxford University Press 1988

Mumford, Lewis, *The City in History*, Harcourt Brace & World 1961

Nijkamp, Peter and Perrels, Adrian, *Sustainable Cities in Europe*, Earthscan Publications 1994

Ohmae, Kenichi, *The Borderless World*, Fontana 1990

Papanek, Victor, *The Green Imperative*, Thames and Hudson 1995

Pearce, David, *Blueprint I, II and III – Measuring Sustainable Development*, Earthscan 1993–7

Pearce, David; Markandya, April and Barbier, Edward B., *Blueprint for a Green Economy*, Earthscan Publications 1989

Ponting, Clive, *The Green History of the World*, St Martin's Press 1991

Porter, Roy, *London – A Social History*, Harvard University Press 1995

Reich, Robert B., *The Work of Nations – A Blueprint for the Future*, Simon and Schuster 1991

Rifkin, Jermey, *The End of Work: The Decline of the Global Labour Force and the Dawn of the Post-Market Era*, G. P. Putnam's Sons, New York 1995

Rogers, Richard and Fisher, Mark, *A New London*, Penguin 1992

Sennett, Richard, *The Fall of Public Man*, Faber and Faber 1974

Seymour, John and Girardet, Herbert, *Blueprint for a Green Planet*, Dorling Kindersley 1987

Sherlock, Harley, *Cities Are Good For Us*, Paladin 1991

Sorkin, Michael, *Exquisite Corpse*, Verso 1991

Thompson, William Irwin, *Gaia II – Emergence. The New Science of Becoming*, Lindisfarne Press 1991

Turner, R. Kerry; Pearce, David and Bateman, Ian, *Environmental Economics, An Elementary Introduction*, Harvester Wheatsheaf 1994

Ward, Barbara, *Progress for a Small Planet*, Penguin 1979

Ward, Barbara and Dubos, René, *Only One Earth*, Penguin 1972

Wilks, Stuart (ed.), *Talking About Tomorrow*, Pluto Press Collection 1993

Williams, Raymond, *The Country and the City*, Hogarth Press 1973

Index

Italic type indicates an illustration or its caption.

Biographies

Richard Rogers was born in Florence, Italy, in 1933 and trained as an architect in London and the USA. An RIBA gold medallist, he is best known for such pioneering buildings as the Centre Georges Pompidou in Paris and Lloyd's of London, and for large-scale master-planning projects in Shanghai, Berlin and London. Previously Chairman of the Tate trustees and Vice-Chair of the Arts Council of England, he remains Chairman of the National Tenants' Resource Centre and the Architecture Foundation. He has been awarded the Légion d'honneur, and was knighted in 1991 for his contributions to artchitecture. He was made a life peer in 1996.

Sir Crispin Tickell is Warden of Green College, Oxford, and Convenor of the Governmental Panel on Sustainable Development. He was Permanent Secretary of the Overseas Development Administration and British Permanent Representative to the United Nations. He has advised successive Prime Ministers on environmental issues, and is the author of *Climatic Change and World Affairs* as well as of numerous articles and lectures on the subject.

Philip Gumuchdjian is Associate Director at the Richard Rogers Partnership. He collaborated on the 'London as It Could Be' proposals exhibited at the Royal Academy in 1986 and on Richard Rogers' Reith Lectures, and was Rapporteur for 'Cities in the 21st Century' at the United Nations Habitat II Conference in Istanbul.